C000064686

OUR MONEY, OUR MOVEMENT

OUR MONEY, OUR MOVEMENT

Building a poor people's credit union

ALANA ALBEE and NANDASIRI GAMAGE

INTERMEDIATE TECHNOLOGY PUBLICATIONS 1996

Intermediate Technology Publications Ltd,
103–105 Southampton Row, London, WC1B 4HH, UK

© Intermediate Technology Publications 1996

A CIP record for this book is available from the British Library

ISBN 1 85339 388 6

Photographs: K.A. Ratnasiri
Illustrations: Chitral Jayasooriya
Typeset by Dorwyn Ltd, Rowlands Castle, Hants and
Printed in UK by SRP Exeter

Contents

ACKNOWLEDGEMENTS   vii

PREFACE   ix

FOREWORD by Diana Mitlin, *International Institute for Environment and Development*   xi

1 The Canal Bank: A short story   1

2 Supporting Emerging Poor People's Organizations   6

3 The Credit Union Co-operative Society   9
    3.1 Background to the Credit Union Movement   9
    3.2 The Women's Credit Union in Sri Lanka   10
    3.3 A Step-by-Step Approach to Group Formation   20
    3.4 When Things Go Wrong   25

4 More than Money: Social development and housing activities   29
    4.1 The Children's Cultural Programme   29
    4.2 Housing Loans   31
    4.3 Additional Social Support   32

5 Towards Sustainability and Scaling-up   34

6 Conclusion   36

NOTES   38

APPENDICES:
    1 Sri Lanka: A situation analysis   39
    2 The Women's Credit Union: Statistical overview, December 1994   43
    3 The Women's Credit Union: Statistical overview of finance, December 1994   44
    4 The *Praja Sahayaka Sewaya* and the Million Houses Programme: Background information   45

BIBLIOGRAPHY   46

Acknowledgements

First and foremost we would like to thank the many low-income people of Sri Lanka who were the source of inspiration, ideas and information contained in this document. Although they may indeed be materially 'poor', they are rich in spirit and commitment. This is their story, and the authors have documented their efforts.

We are also grateful to The Arkleton Trust who provided funds without which this piece of work would have been much longer in the making, and to the Swedish International Development Corporation Agency for their support in publishing the book.

Particular thanks to Professor Sirasena Tilakaratna whose commitment to participatory processes is second to none and whose ability to reveal and clearly describe complex processes has helped us enormously.

Finally, special thanks to Graham Boyd whose encouragement, analytical thinking and probing questions have supported not only the production of this document but the development of a poor people's organization.

ALANA ALBEE
Midmills Road
Inverness, Scotland

NANDASIRI GAMAGE
Community leader
Community Resource Centre
Borella, Colombo
Sri Lanka

Preface

The emergence of low-income people's organizations in Sri Lanka has had a chequered history. The case presented in this book represents a small but significant shift in the way the urban poor have been able to instigate, own and multiply their own development process. It represents a break from more conventional development approaches in which community activists and organizations are participants in externally controlled State and NGO development programmes.

A decade of more conventional development has, in some instances, brought out leadership qualities in low-income individuals. These individuals have gained experience in acting in roles such as health volunteers or leaders of local groups such as community development councils. However, their lasting impact has been limited. The local groups have stumbled along for a time but eventually many have withered away. Such interventions and organizational structures are not initiated by low-income people themselves and therefore have not had the strength of purpose, motivation and creative energy to survive beyond the period of external assistance. Some of the individuals involved have, however, become subsequently involved in locally driven initiatives such as the credit union described in this document.

The women's credit union in Sri Lanka has several important features that set it apart from other development initiatives. The first is its urban nature. Rural credit programmes have achieved considerable success and have been well documented; there have been fewer examples of urban successes. The very transient and heterogeneous nature of urban dwellers makes any assistance a complex and uneven process.

Valuable lessons can be gained from this document that provides technical details about how it was developed and how it functions.

Another unique aspect of this credit union is its recognition of the important role of poor urban women. It has supported them to overcome their isolation, first through small pre-cooperative groups and then through federating into a credit union. The fact that it initially mirrored traditional credit in Sri Lanka enabled women to grasp and own the concept quickly. It emphasized the use of verbal training methods, social preparation, exposure visits, group solidarity and the development of a cadre of internal facilitators. The social preparation and mobilization through the creation of two facilitative organizations, the PSS (Community Agent Service) and then the KSS (Women's Support Service), have been instrumental to the whole process of building a people's organization. The cost of these services has been provided by external aid and represents value for money in comparison to the higher costs of most State and NGO programmes which utilize project officers and extension workers. There is little hierarchy or social distance in the structure of this credit union in comparison with other credit projects and banking approaches, such as the Grameen Bank in Bangladesh.

Finally, this credit union illustrates that poor people can begin to make significant and sustainable progress if given the encouragement, support and freedom to act as the agents of their own development. However, the progress is often constrained by their own limited horizons. The challenges facing this credit union will be whether they can build and synchronize several parts of the credit mechanism as it grows over the coming years. These include horizontal expansion to reach critical mass by drawing in more new members, quality technical development through accessing experienced external professional guidance, and vertical expansion through stimulating further carefully planned loan stages for mature members.

GRAHAM BOYD
Technical Adviser, formerly with the United Nations Centre for Human Settlements

Foreword

In virtually all cities in Africa, Asia and Latin America, a large proportion of low-income residents have to construct their own housing and often have to develop their own roads, drains and other forms of infrastructure. This process, and the broader urbanization process of which it is part, have often been portrayed in a negative light. However, the work of the *Kantha Sahayaka Sewaya* (or Women's Credit Union in Sri Lanka) demonstrates the vision, hard work, skills, patience and perseverance of low-income communities living in urban areas of Sri Lanka as they seek to secure and improve their livelihoods and to obtain adequate housing. Through the development of savings schemes and small-scale credit, they have been able to strengthen local organizations and livelihood opportunities. It is only through understanding and building on activities like these that development assistance agencies and governments can develop and support an improved model of urban development that responds to the needs and energies of low-income citizens.

Urban poverty: a growing problem?

People's organizations such as those described in this book reflect the growing interest that UN agencies, governments and NGOs show in working with the urban poor. The women's credit union described here grew out of a larger programme of activity in 1989 which involved both the Sri Lankan government and United Nations agencies. These and other new initiatives have arisen more from an increased awareness of the problems of the urban poor than from any evident changes in the scale of urban poverty. A further factor is the recognition that,

by 2005, more than half of the world's population is expected to live in urban areas; and that ten years later, by 2015, this will include the majority of those living in the South (United Nations, 1995).

There are no accurate figures for the proportion of the world's population who live in poverty in urban areas, even if a simple income-based poverty line is used to estimate this. However, it is hard to find any detailed national or city study where less than one-quarter of the urban population have incomes below the poverty line (Tabatabai, 1993). A number of studies have suggested that urban poverty is growing, particularly as a result of the measures taken by structural adjustment programmes. Estimates of the scale of poverty based on the number of people living in very poor housing and lacking such basic services as piped water, provision for sanitation and garbage collection, and access to health care may be more realistic than estimates based on incomes. At least 600 million urban dwellers in Africa, Asia and Latin America are estimated to live in 'life- and health-threatening' homes and neighbourhoods (Cairncross, Hardoy and Satterthwaite, 1990).

In many towns and cities, these residents are struggling to make best use of their limited resources to improve their situation. This document illustrates an example of how they have been able to do so effectively.

Savings and credit groups like those described in this report are particularly important in addressing the needs of low-income groups. Within urban centres, inadequate incomes are a major cause of poverty, but it is inadequate assets which underlie low-income groups' vulnerability to economic shocks or to the economic consequences of ill-health (Chambers, 1995; Pryer, 1993). It is often economic vulnerability to a sudden crisis that moves a household from being able to (just) meet their needs into becoming destitute. Pryer (1993) describes the difficult situation faced by low-income urban households in Khulna, Bangladesh, when faced with illness. Without community-based insurance and credit schemes which would enable them to meet the costs of health care and to compensate for the loss of income, the families were forced into debt. Lack of income resulted in under-nourishment (among adults and children) and continuing health problems, and a further loss of income. Small funds, such as those created and managed by *Kantha Sahayaka Sewaya*, prevent a single difficult event from having such severe consequences.

Women often have particular difficulties in gaining access to income, resources and services. Differentials may occur within households, between male and female household members, or between households, with women-headed households at a disadvantage relative to male-headed households. Among low-income households, those headed by women usually face particular problems in that they experience discrimination in finding work, in securing support for income-generating activities or household improvements and in having to combine the triple role of child-rearing, household (and community) maintenance, and income generation (Moser, 1993). In many low-income settlements, a significant proportion of households are headed by women either because a male partner is temporarily absent or because of separation or death (Moser, 1987). There are also generally significant income differentials between men and women related to the types of occupation available to them, pay rates within occupations and, for entrepreneurs, access to credit.

Savings and loan programmes focusing on women have developed to address the discrimination faced by women in running their own enterprises and, therefore, in developing their business opportunities. Many have used the structures favoured by the women's credit union, that is small groups coming together to better realize their individual needs. As has been the case in Sri Lanka, in many countries this has provided a base from which to expand activities, both to federate individual groups (and their savings) into larger institutions and to expand from credit to other activities in order to meet the multiple needs of low-income urban households.

Urban development and poverty reduction strategies

Governments in the South have used many different approaches to improve housing and living conditions for low-income groups over the past 25–30 years, most of which have had limited success. In the past two decades, it has become increasingly evident that programmes which work with local development initiatives are among the most effective means through which governments can support a pattern of urban development which favours low-income households. In several countries, including Sri Lanka, governments have been attempting to put in place such programmes.

In Sri Lanka, the Million Houses Programme, together with its precursor and successor the Hundred Thousand Houses Programme and the Million and a Half Houses Programme, has sought to address the country's housing programme in both rural and urban areas. In urban areas, the government had a clear strategy of supporting an incremental development process in low-income settlements and of working with local residents through a joint planning process. The central role of community organizations was recognized through the creation of (and support for) community development councils. The training programme included workshops to strengthen the councils, information on land regularization and building guidelines, and assistance in establishing women's enterprise support for savings and credit (Sirivardana, 1994). A further innovation was the introduction of community construction contracts within which the community development councils were responsible for managing small-scale infrastructure construction work. This had the dual advantage of providing the councils with finance and ensuring the use of informal construction labour in settlement improvements.

In Sri Lanka, the government attempted to ensure that improved housing was integral to the vision of poverty alleviation (Sirivardana, 1994). In this respect, the government showed an unusual commitment to improved housing for low-income communities in urban and rural areas. Few governments make such commitments, or are as successful in putting in place programmes which result in real improvements on a significant scale. More recently, the government has also sought to provide more direct income support through the *Jansaviya* Programme. One component deals directly with the issue of insufficient investment capacity within the informal sector through a savings and small loans programme for income generation (Sirivardana, 1994).

Understanding what governments cannot do

Experiences with such innovative programmes have led to a much clearer understanding of what governments can and cannot do. The style and operation of government departments often make it difficult for their staff to work directly with communities. There are problems of information, understanding, local management and commitment. Without good information about community concerns, government staff are unable to identify the interventions preferred by community members. If programmes are not based within representative community organizations, the benefits of development projects may be enjoyed by the wealthier and better connected people within the settlement. If local residents do not feel a sense of ownership over the project, then the benefits are unlikely to be maintained. For example, infrastructure will not be repaired and repayments to local loan funds will be avoided if possible.

A further problem, and perhaps one of the greatest problems within government programmes, has been that of dependency. The support that programme beneficiaries have received from government encourages them to believe that government is willing and able to address their needs. In nearly every case, the infrastructure and other services provided are partial, inadequate in scale and of poor quality. However, the promise of more to come makes it difficult to organize and mobilize local residents to address their own needs either directly or through putting pressure on the state. Within the Million Houses Programme, an acknowledged problem was that some of the community development councils acted simply to distribute government services, and this reduced their role to one of reinforcing dependency on the state (UNCHS, 1993). This process not only reduces the level of community activity but, over time, reduces residents' confidence in their own ability to identify and resolve problems.

Without a strong local organization, it is difficult for low-income residents to be able to address the multiple disadvantages they face. In the case of *Kantha Sahayaka Sewaya*, residents in the community have pooled their savings and created a capital fund through which they are able to invest in micro-enterprises and increase their incomes. In low-income settlements throughout the world, collective activity is the basis for improved well-being and opportunity. In Buenos Aires (Argentina), women have supported a child-care centre with voluntary labour, financial contributions and fund-raising to provide better health care and education for their children. In Fortaleza (Brazil), women and men have collectively constructed houses in order to improve the quality of their accommodation. In Dar es Salaam (Tanzania), residents form night patrols to reduce the risk of crime. In Karachi (Pakistan), households have collectively planned for lane sanitation in order to improve environmental conditions. Without such activity, residents are unable to make efficient use of the resources that they have.

As noted at the beginning of the book, the significance of organizations such as *Kantha Sahayaka Sewaya* is that they have succeeded in articulating and developing strategies that are rooted in poor people's lives and have a capacity to realize tangible and sustained improvements in the well-being of individuals and households. Organizations like these offer an alternative vision based on realizing the strength of local structures and capacities, and building development organizations based on these strengths. As the authors of this report argue, fundamental to the success of the community workers has been 'their belief in the abilities of others and their willingness to share opportunities and power with other poor people'.

Unlike many other initiatives, the women's credit union described here has developed with little external assistance and for that reason it is of particular interest. It has emerged from an independent group of community development workers (from low-income settlements) who were first employed within the Million Houses Programme and who decided that they could work more effectively outside the government agencies (Gamage, 1993). As discussed in Chapter 2, external agencies need to carefully consider how to foster a people-centred development process.

Savings and credit

Experiences throughout the world over the past 20 years have demonstrated the central role played by the provision of credit within programmes to improve livelihoods for low-income households. Without opportunities for savings and loans, it is not possible to use existing resources effectively. This is evident in a number of contexts:

○ **Income**: credit is needed for all manner of livelihood activities both for investment in equipment and for bulk purchase of essential inputs.
○ **Expenditure**: access to credit enables the small amount of money available to be used efficiently. With respect to housing, a lack of credit means that improvements are inefficient and have to be repaired many times at additional cost. Later developments, such as a second storey, may require the demolition and reconstruction of earlier building work.
○ **Emergency**: a lack of finance in emergencies can be sufficient to push a low-income household into the category of very poor.

The focus on rural development has resulted in many projects and programmes that are concerned with the provision of credit in rural areas. However, there is now a growing interest in similar initiatives in urban areas. Hurley (1990) describes a range of interventions undertaken by external agencies to support the informal sector in urban areas, including credit programmes, greater access to markets (for example, through the legalization of street traders), and the provision of vocational training.

As in the case of *Kantha Sahayaka Sewaya*, micro-enterprise programmes are being linked to housing and neighbourhood development programmes. This development has taken place with the dual extension of micro-enterprise to housing and from housing to micro-enterprise. The Grameen Bank, for example, is one of the best known examples of micro-enterprise lending. It has also provided 290,000 housing loans using lending mechanisms established for its more traditional activities

(Anzorena, 1994). The loan is for a standard package of building materials costing about US$300. SPARC, an NGO in Bombay, has been involved in housing-related community development activities for many years. While establishing a loan fund for housing, the women's groups that it was working with also chose to set up a fund for emergencies and micro-enterprise lending (Patel and d'Cruz, 1993). In both cases, these developments have taken place because the multiple needs of low-income groups are closely linked, and programmes that respond to local priorities have to deal with a range of diverse activities.

Housing finance

The housing activities of the *Kantha Sahayaka Sewaya* remain limited but they reflect the need for households to have access to housing finance. Women wish to invest in their houses to improve their businesses and to create an asset. Without such finance, housing expenditure is wasteful and inefficient. Construction is incremental and the disruption is great; walls that have been constructed one year have to be replaced as the house grows because they are not strong enough to bear the weight of the next storey. Only small quantities of materials can be afforded and unit costs are greater.

There is an increasing number of NGOs trying to raise the necessary capital to establish funds for housing finance. As in Sri Lanka, they are motivated by the evident household requirements for loan capital for housing investment, and the lack of government activity in this area. One of the reasons why governments are reluctant to provide such financing is that they have been unsuccessful in obtaining repayments. However, experience suggests that working with organizations such as *Kantha Sahayaka Sewaya* may prove to be a more effective route for governments seeking both to support low-income communities and obtain an agreed level of repayments.

Within Sri Lanka, limited government finance for housing developments has previously been made available but the experiences have been problematic. Between 1985 and 1992, 34,000 houses were constructed in urban areas with loans from the Million Houses Programme. The programme also provided technical advice for house building and thereby assisted a further 50,000 households. There were many problems associated with these housing loans delivered by government, including the selection of beneficiaries, a lack of flexibility in the guarantee system, heavy administration and complex repayment systems (ESCAP, 1991). One early conclusion from the government programme was that repayments were more successfully managed through co-operatives with collective loan management. However, a continuing difficulty has been that politicians prefer to give rather than receive repayments! (UNCHS, 1993).

Experiences from other countries have identified a number of problems associated with housing finance programmes delivered through government agencies. Governments lack information on households and find it difficult to make accurate decisions about applicants. Many loan recipients do not expect to repay debts to government. And many government agencies are not suited to working directly with low-income households or community organizations; their style is bureaucratic, their offices inconveniently located and open at the wrong times, and their collateral and security arrangements designed for those in formal sector employment. Community groups and NGOs have sought to address the lack of provision for housing loans directly. But many face major difficulties in obtaining sufficient capital, and this is also an evident constraint for *Kantha Sahayaka Sewaya*.

Conclusion

It is evident that the official process of urban development has not met the needs of low-income communities or supported the processes through which the unofficial cities are being constructed. In Sri Lanka, many urban communities and their organizations still retain a confidence that governments will meet their needs for infrastructure and services. However, they are increasingly looking to better manage and direct their own resources in order to develop local economies and improve their housing. The needs of many urban and rural residents are similar and it is not surprising that the women's credit union has seen its activities extend to rural areas. The approaches described in the report have drawn on other experiences but they have avoided the simple adoption of models developed elsewhere.

At every stage, the process and structure of the savings and credit union have to make sense to the women who manage the process and who benefit from the pooling of resources. In addition to securing increased incomes (through loans for micro-enterprises) and more efficient expenditure (through housing finance), the programme has also responded to a demand to revitalize cultural traditions within low-income areas. By rooting the development of the organization with small-level organizations, the members of the credit union have sought to ensure that they have control over the bank they are creating and the organization they are participating in, in order to ensure that both institutions continue to meet their needs and serve their interests. In this report, they discuss their experiences and thereby make this information available to others.[1]

The hardest lesson for all external agencies is the realization of how little they can do. Without local support, their programmes become irrelevant or detrimental to those they are seeking to help. Through alliances with people's organizations, such agencies have an opportunity to contribute to local residents' self-determined development. It is the history and experience of one such initiative that is described in the following pages.

DIANA MITLIN
*International Institute for Environment
and Development*

---

[1] Considerable interest has already been shown in the activities of *Kantha Sahayaka Sewaya*. The programme was recently the site of a workshop of the Training and Advisory Programme of the Asian Coalition for Housing Rights (for more information contact TAP-ACHR, 73 Soi Sonthiwattana 4, Ladprao 110, Ladprao Rd, Bangkok 10310, Thailand).

1

The Canal Bank: A short story

This story was written by Nandasiri Gamage, a community leader from one low-income area of Colombo. Translated from Sinhala, it describes life in a canal bank shanty and the people's frustrated aspirations. It was written to give the reader an insight into life in Colombo.

The stagnant pungent smelling water from the canal flows under the rusty Wellawatta Bridge in the centre of Colombo. It carries thick layers of oil, dirt and light debris accumulated after passing through several slum areas of the city. The heavier particles sink gradually through the black water and eventually settle on the murky canal bed, adding to the layers of old tins, rusted iron and human waste.

Like all the canal banks and the shore of Colombo Lake, these banks are a dumping ground. They are crowded with shanties. Everything that is not used by the city dwellers is discarded here, not in the rarely found Municipal Council rubbish bins, but in the canal. Whatever is thrown into the canal seems to be light and weightless as it bobs dolefully in the thick water. The occasional white egret easily catches a lifeless fish that comes to the surface for a breath of fresh air. Boys with jutting bellies like watermelons answer the call of nature on the canal bank, throwing all that is within reach into the canal as they squat and defecate. A used coconut thrown by one boy gradually sinks into the layers of slime making the sound, 'boosshhh'. Black bubbles that emerge spread and pop on the surface.

The people who live in the wooden and tin-roofed shacks on the banks of the canal have so much aspiration. They are like the bubbles emerging from the depths of mud, slowly rising to the surface. But like the bubbles popping when exposed to the elements, their aspirations fade away. Their lives have been digested by the canal banks like the used coconut embraced by the mud.

Early every morning Jayatunga rides his bike along the dusty canal bank road, shouting "Fiiish . . . Fiiish". This is his life. He earns his living in this way. Living in the slums near the canal he sells his fish to willing buyers easily found in the shacks of the shanties.

For years Jayatunga has followed the same daily pattern, claiming the canal bank as his territory. "Hey brother, this is my route, okay!" he shouts to a colleague who attempts to sell fish on the same road. Although his tone is harsh and threatening the other knows he is only half serious.

It was on one of these days when he was selling fish that Jayatunga met Mallika. Her mother and father, both daily labourers earning a meagre wage, toil all day carrying sand and bricks to build castles for the rich. Their lives revolve around the rich both during the day and at night when they lay on their bed of mats in their leaky shanty and dream about the long day to come.

Mallika's parents could not afford to pay for her education so, to make herself useful, Mallika helps her parents by caring for her younger brothers and sisters. She often buys fish from Jayatunga, and lately he has begun to sell fish cheaply to her. There is a reason for it, and it is no secret among the people living in the area. Jayatunga united in the world of love with Mallika, and in time Jayatunga's small cardboard palace appeared among the shacks of the shanty area. Shanties appear like roots bursting out of a banana bush. The shoots which could not be seen in the bunch yesterday stand out today like a straightened sword.

Jayatunga the fish seller

Jayatunga still gets his meagre earnings from selling fish on his bicycle along the canal route, but soon he believes he will start his fish business in his own hut with his wife helping him. The government has started filling the marshy area on the opposite side of the canal bank and new roads have been constructed. Now many vehicles can be seen travelling at great speed and trailing long columns of dust behind them. The aspirations of Jayatunga and others living on the opposite side of the canal bank were immediately influenced by these activities.

For many evenings Mallika eagerly watched the construction on the opposite bank. One day, while enjoying the treat of a raw woodapple, she could no longer resist the temptation of feeling the new world with the soles of her bare feet, and so she strolled over with her unborn child. A Pajero four-wheel drive vehicle sped down the road, coating Mallika with dust. A soldier travelling in the jeep stuck out his tongue aggressively at her. Mallika, enraged, repeated the rude gesture and threw the piece of woodapple shell at the vehicle. Mocking laughter rang in Mallika's ears.

"People say the Mayor has built a new bungalow at the end of the new land and has moved in!" Mallika told Jayatunga immediately when he arrived home.

"Which Mayor?" Jayatunga asked while cleaning the spokes of his bicycle.

"I don't know which Mayor. Dabare and a few others were talking and I happened to hear. I suppose it would be a high ranking person after seeing the big vehicles going up and down the road. It is now called 'Canal Drive'."

"Probably the name of some white man," said Jayatunga, scraping the rust off the wheels.

"There are rumours that we will be given houses very soon. Then we won't have to live in these leaky shacks any more."

"What good news!" said Jayatunga excitedly.

"I think this comes with the good fortune of expecting a child," Mallika said dreamily.

"But are we going to get a card from the Housing Authority?" asked Jayatunga cautiously.

"We will get a plot of land from my mother's card," said Mallika, not wanting the excitement to be dampened.

"We must have a separate house for ourselves!" insisted Jayatunga.

Both Jayatunga and Mallika continued to discuss the future in excited but hushed voices until late into the night. The earth fillings and the levelled land on the opposite side of the canal emitted a golden aura and glittered in the moonlight. The oil lamps hanging in the shanty huts were dimmed by the brightness of the moon.

Like the sound of electric thunder, the Pajero boomed down the new road. "Jaya . . . there he goes, the great Mayor!" Mallika said hastily. When Jayatunga looked into the distance he only saw the silhouette of the fearsome vehicles.

"We should get houses soon."

"Why is that?" Mallika questioned.

"I doubt that these blue-blooded people want to see this kind of hell when they drive to their homes. Do you think they will want to have these shacks forever in front of their eyes?"

"But would they demolish our huts and drive away?'

"No, that won't happen," said Jayatunga confidently. "Dabare knows we voted for his Lordship the Mayor in the last election."

"Dabare may know, but does his Lordship?" asked Mallika.

"Why not? Dabare always said that his Lordship the Mayor sees the people on the canal bank as his."

"Then Dabare must have told the Mayor we voted for him in the last election," Mallika stated, renewing her confidence.

"Yes . . . yes, the Mayor has said he would find a solution to our problem as soon as possible," confirmed Jayatunga.

"Thank god! What good news!" said Mallika excitedly.

"We should get a plan drawn up by Mr Weerasingha," suggested Jayatunga.

Mallika, not knowing who Mr Weerasingha was, asked about him.

"A gentleman to whom I sell fish," was the reply. "His home is like paradise: complete with streams and ponds with golden coloured fish. The garden is like a jungle haven with soft grass. He draws plans."

Mallika stared at him, open mouthed. She felt a surge of satisfaction, then she suddenly felt worried for herself, thinking that she would never have the fortune of such a house. "A small house is sufficient for us," she said quietly.

"Yes, a verandah, a room, and a kitchen is more than enough," Jayatunga reassured her.

"A toilet should be attached to the house," she added hastily.

Jayatunga smiled looking at her expectant stomach, fluorescent in the moonlight.

"The dew is very strong, let's go inside," he took her by the hand and led her inside.

The news they received the next morning was enough to destroy their castle in the air. The police had given an order to demolish their shanty within one week.

3

The canal bank

"This is a thundering crime. Where do they want us to go, leaving this haven?" shouted Jayatunga as he re-wrapped his sarong.

Dabare had arrived and tried to calm the confusion, saying "Don't shout, brother. We will not give in and not a single house will be destroyed. I have already discussed this with His Lordship the Mayor the day the order was given."

"Oh, I see." Jayatunga sighed, as his temper began to cool.

Two weeks later Jayatunga's familiar voice shouting "Fiiish . . . fiiish" stopped abruptly. He saw the shocking scene of people surrounding the vehicles of the police and municipal workers like bees from a disturbed hive. Dabare was running here and there leading the crowd. He twisted like a worm pulled out of his element. He explained facts and figures to the Head of Police.

"It is not our wish to destroy your houses, but the order has come from the top," the Head of Police explained.

One by one, like a herd of wild elephants destroying a well matured civilization, the police started breaking up the shanties. Planks and tin sheets flew to the ground making the sound of fire-crackers.

"From the top?" shouted Dabare. "Top in the sense of below the Mayor, right? This is a big mistake. His Lordship the Mayor would never allow such a thing."

Dabare grabbed a nearby bicycle and raced along Canal Drive. His unbuttoned shirt waved like a flag and his chest exposed to the rushing wind.

The others gathered in the temple, having grabbed from their huts the 'wealth' most close to their lives: clothing, identity cards and rice ration coupons. The temple swarmed with people.

"The Mayor has left Sri Lanka on official business. In the meantime some villain has done this . . . this dirty work," seethed Dabare. He got off the bicycle and dropped the contents of the official file onto the ground.

4

"Gone abroad, setting the trap . . ." said a voice.

"Don't talk rubbish, Gunapala," barked Dabare angrily.

"Dirty work is good, words are bad," Gunapala told Dabare as he helped him pick up the scattered documents.

The expressions of the others showed their mixed emotions of sadness and fright. Uncertain, they looked to Dabare for leadership. "We shall stay in the temple until the Mayor comes back to Sri Lanka. Then we shall find a solution to this problem. We can't let things like this happen!" Dabare said ultimately.

"You idiot Dabare! Can't you see how they've tread quietly over us. You do the slavery for them. We don't have the right to land in our own country. We are branded as 'unauthorized'. As a matter of fact our whole generation is unauthorized, isn't that so! Look, slave Dabare, the blue-blooded people have everything! Yes, everything is authorized for them. For us, everything is unauthorized. Someday you will understand the truth! Only then come and talk to me!" Gunapala's voice echoed for a long time in Dabare's ears.

Jayatunga and Mallika were among the refugees that night in the temple; Mallika felt labour pains. Jayatunga took her to the government maternity home assisted by her elderly mother.

"We may bring the baby back to the temple," Jayatunga told his mother-in-law as they returned from the hospital. "It is a good omen for the baby's first visit to be to the temple," he said with irony.

2

Supporting Emerging Poor People's Organizations

Jayatunga and his wife, in the short story in Chapter 1, had aspirations to obtain a small piece of housing land and basic amenities but these were frustrated by their status and individualized efforts. As isolated individuals they were powerless to influence the government and municipal delivery systems in their favour and were also unable to influence those who determined land allocations and services. Any problem-solving potential of their existing community organization was overshadowed by party political alliances.

Jayatunga and his wife illustrate how isolated individuals and families tend to become defeated in their efforts and accept the status quo as their fate. Empirical evidence shows that the poor often display an awareness of their situation but their social behaviour is characterized by inaction. How can this be overcome? Collective action and solidarity is an important empowering mechanism. By forming a collective identity for taking action, people can better seek to address their aspirations.

In its broadest sense, the purpose of an organization is to provide a continuing mechanism for the pursuit of the interests of its members as collectively identified by them.[1]

The poor become active agents in their own process of development through forming their own organizations. This does not, however, happen spontaneously. In many communities there are traditional forms of collective action such as savings clubs, funeral aid societies and exchange of labour during cultivation and harvest. However, these activities do not address the core issue of poverty and dependence. They have not led to the generation of sustained action by the poor to change such conditions and to improve their status. **The rationale for supporting the growth of poor people's organizations is rooted in the reality that sustained action directed at issues of poverty and dependence rarely takes place spontaneously.**

Supporting the growth of poor people's organizations requires a coherent and rigorous approach which enables the poor to become active agents of their own development. It involves assisting the collective poor to gather information about their circumstances and resources, to analyse their situation, to prioritize actions they wish to pursue, and to work out the means of implementing this action. This is done through a systematic process of action-reflection-action, and as such it is continuous and shifting. Each step unfolds the subsequent steps thus creating a self-propelled dynamic. This, where appropriately supported by outside professionals, often leads to a chain of interconnected actions.

This approach to development contrasts sharply with the more conventional approach of centrally conceived and managed project or programme planning. In the conventional approach, inputs and outputs are pre-set and rigidly established before implementation. Parameters such as project objectives, targets and indicators are defined and determined in detail. These become the benchmarks for gauging impact and effectiveness, and determine the methods used in project implementation and evaluation. Parameters which are specific, time-bound and measurable are viewed as most desirable.[2] This conventional and professionalized development approach leaves little scope for the emergence of new ideas, creativity and experimentation by the poor themselves.

Such frequently promoted elitist development approaches are driven by products rather than processes.

The roots of these rigid planning processes reflect their origins in large-scale engineering and manufacturing projects. Many of the techniques have been adopted by social development workers in the hopes of minimizing risk and ensuring financial accountability. They are, however, ill-suited to the social development process in which human growth and empowerment issues are of central importance.

How can support be given to the emergence of poor people's organizations? If the objective is to support sustainable organizations which are democratically owned and controlled, then the role of development workers and agencies must change. The development workers' role should become less conventional than is generally the case to date. They should no longer be the experts who know best. They should be out of the limelight and function only in the shadow of the organized poor, allowing the poor themselves to control the process. The *Bhoomi Sena* (Land Army) movement in India explains it this way:

An outsider who comes with ready-made solutions is worse than useless. He must first understand from us what our questions are, and help us articulate the questions better, and then help us find solutions. Outsiders also have to change. He alone is a friend who helps us think about our problems on our own.[3]

Such a 'support role' focuses on animation and facilitation. Animation helps to raise awareness of problems; facilitation assists groups to overcome practical barriers in problem solving. The external worker draws out potential options and difficulties during the process, and learns with the poor, exercising influence but not control. This influencing role is sometimes misinterpreted as manipulation; the difference is rooted in the issue of trust. Influencing is a flexible, transparent and open process; manipulation is not.

The need for animation and facilitation is clearly explained by Professor Tilakaratna:

Animation is necessary but not necessarily a sufficient condition to enable the poor to undertake and manage collective action to transform their reality. There are a host of factors which operate to keep them passive rather than active. Given their deep-rooted dependence and submission . . . and lack of experience in initiating and managing collective actions, it may take time before they develop confidence in their abilities to bring about change. While animation by breaking mental barriers begins to show possibilities for change, facilitation is a task of assisting the poor to break the practical barriers to action. External intervenors with their formal education, wider knowledge of social contexts, social contacts and status derived from affiliation to a formal organization such as a 'development agency' are able to act as resource persons to people's groups to help overcome some of their practical problems.[4]

Facilitation[5] may include the following:
○ support for acquiring basic management and technical skills;
○ assistance to people's groups to develop contacts with formal institutions, agencies and bureaucracies;
○ participatory training in planning and building strategies for their organization;
○ clearing obstacles imposed by power structures and creating space for poor people's actions to grow; providing an initial phase of protection and encouragement.

This approach enables learning to take place as the process unfolds; shared learning leading to shared ownership, not by the funders or professional development workers, but by the poor themselves who are the doers and evaluators. This is the foundation of a people's organization.

Support through facilitation and animation cannot be strictly time-bound, and this is where conventional project planning approaches break down. Projecting the number of years required to build the capacity of any group of collective poor is extremely difficult. What can be said, however, is that it does not result in quick or immediately measurable results.

A crucial sign of progress is the increasing redundancy of the external animator/facilitator. This implies a recognition by poor people of their own abilities and autonomy. It involves both a weaning process and an assertion of self-determination by the poor. The importance of external animators/facilitators becoming redundant is clearly expressed by a community worker in the Philippines:

> *It is easy to forget that . . . development animators themselves can become a major stumbling block . . . We (the animators) sometimes become unaware of our own tendency to impose our biases, values, visions, and attitudes on the people.*[6]

Woven into this progressive redundancy is the building up of an internal cadre of local activists who are intricately involved and committed to collective action and building poor peoples' organizations. The role of these people is to encourage and support local participation. Fundamental to their success is their belief in the abilities of others and their willingness to share opportunities and power with other poor people.

It is the collective and co-operative aspects of this people-centred development approach which fundamentally differentiates it from institution building. It focuses on building the capacity of the poor to identify societal constraints and their own needs, to manage their own development, and to form themselves into sustainable and transparent local organizations. Its objective is to work towards people's organizations based on solidarity and common democratic ownership. This contrasts with 'institution building' which by definition focuses on creating centralized hierarchies without common ownership by the poor.

3

The Credit Union Co-operative Society

This chapter provides technical information on credit unions generally, and the women's credit union in Sri Lanka most particularly. It is an illustration of how the poor can manage their own resources and build their own organization.

There was no 'master plan' which guided the building of the poor women's credit union in Sri Lanka. It was a process which evolved over several years and was based on key principles which guide all credit unions (see below). Many of the people involved studied other credit and savings initiatives, such as the Grameen Bank (Bangladesh) and Thrift and Credit Co-operative Societies. They then incorporated elements into a system which meets their particular needs.

The approach purposely avoided transferring a 'model' of credit and savings to the Sri Lankan poor. As an alternative, women were encouraged and supported to build their own system. In this way, women's capacity building was as important an objective as developing a mechanism for savings and credit.

3.1 Background to the Credit Union Movement

Credit unions are an important mechanism through which poor people themselves can own and control resources. Credit unions are financial co-operatives which are open to any group of people wishing to save and lend on the basis of a common bond. There are threads which unite credit unions worldwide, but the details of how any given union functions is determined locally. Credit unions most often operate without the bureaucracy and institutional apparatus of centralized and hierarchical organizations such as banks. Worldwide there is an estimated 86 billion individual members of credit unions who belong to more than 40 thousand local affiliates.

Each credit union is a financial co-operative owned and controlled by its members. For poor and disadvantaged people credit unions offer a mechanism for savings and loans unavailable through most formal banking systems. Loans are issued on the basis of accumulated savings. Collateral and complicated form-filling is avoided.

In eight low-income areas of Colombo and twelve rural areas, primary branches of a women's credit union have formed which reach approximately 3600 women. Its formal title is *The Colombo Women's Thrift and Credit Co-operative Society*. It incorporates key elements promoted in many parts of the movement throughout the world. These include:

○ **Decentralized development** in which the *base* of the organization is the heart of activities. This contrasts with a banking approach in which a hierarchy of decision-making and management exists, and where resources are delivered downwards to beneficiaries rather than managed by them.

○ **Saving is promoted** before loans are issued to members. Thus building the self-reliant base of lending capital from the members themselves.

○ **A common bond** between members is emphasized. This bond can form on the basis of living in the same area or of being members of a common profession.

○ **Common ownership** by the members is promoted. This is done through the issuing of shares which are sold to members.

9

Members of the women's credit union, producing breakfast foods for sale

○ **Equity**: voting on the basis of membership not ownership of shares.

3.2 The Women's Credit Union in Sri Lanka

a. Formation

The Colombo women's credit union emerged out of a pilot project initiated by the government in 1989 with support from two United Nations agencies.[7] This pilot project, known initially as Women's Mutual Help Groups, had as its main objective the provision of a mechanism for savings and credit for poor women. It began as a small initiative managed within the then innovative but bureaucratic apparatus of the government's National Housing Development Authority. The project reached approximately 50 women in five low-income areas during its first year.

Several lessons emerged from the Women's Mutual Help Groups pilot project. These included recognition of the importance of:

○ *a solidarity group approach* based on mutual trust among women;

○ individual women having the *freedom to choose whom they joined with* in forming a solidarity group;

○ individual members having the *freedom to choose what productive activity* they undertook:

○ the problems created by a conventional development approach in which there is a significant *social divide between government extension staff and the poor whom they attempt to reach*;

○ *leadership as a crucial factor in the growth of strong groups*. Leaders need to be able to create a sense of cohesion even in times of internal conflict. They require the ability to negotiate arrangements which are fair and equitable to members.

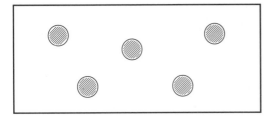

1989
Random isolated credit and savings solidarity groups

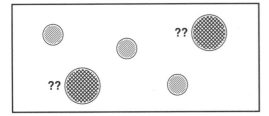

1990
Two groups face near collapse

1991
Federating of groups; key leaders develop
as the KSS support structure

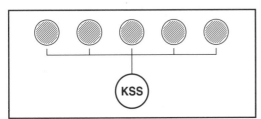

1992
New groups are supported to develop
by the experienced leaders of the KSS

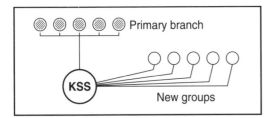

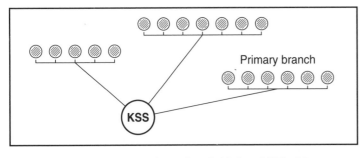

1993
The number of groups
and branches increases

Figure 1 *Development of the Credit Union 1989–93*

Beyond these factors but linked to them was the recognition, in 1990, that free-standing groups not linked to each other were not likely to survive the test of time.

'Federating' or 'joining together' became a crucial means of survival for the groups. This emerged when two of the five groups faced near-collapse (see section 3.4).

11

Federating was seen as a means by which groups could gain strength through solidarity, share their experiences and jointly solve problems. It has enabled members to gather and discuss the lending system and to develop ways of increasing its effectiveness. More recently, federating has also enabled the rapid expansion of the credit union.

The following illustrates the year-by-year development of the Women's Credit Union from isolated groups to federating and developing a support structure known as the KSS (*Kantha Sahayaka Sewaya*).

The KSS is made up of leaders of existing groups. They promote and act as the social mobilizers for the credit union by meeting with new members of potential groups. All KSS members are from low-income areas themselves and are able to explain the process in ways which are easily understood by other women.

b. Organizational structure and primary branches

All the work of this women's credit union is rooted in the activities undertaken at the group level. The groups are the heart of the organization. What makes it unique? The key factor is that all the people involved are poor. The groups as well as the members of the KSS live in areas or settlements which are sometimes referred to as 'slums' or 'shanties'.

The *Kantha Sahayaka Sewaya* (KSS) undertakes the promotion, development and training of the groups. It is a system which is both practical and efficient, as well as comparatively low-cost.

The KSS has a small staff, all of whom are recruited from the members of the groups. Although they have differing functions, the individual KSS staff work as a team with minimal hierarchy.

The KSS supports the formation of groups and primary branches. Primary branches are basically 'mini-banks' made up of approximately eight groups. Section 3.3 outlines the step-by-step process of building groups and primary branches.

As the number of groups and primary branches expand, the KSS also taps the skills of other members in the 'pool' of women mobilizers. These mobilizers work on an ad hoc and part-time basis, as and when required, but are a vital element in the expansion of the movement (see section 3.3). Most women mobilizers are themselves entrepreneurs who sell items in the markets or produce goods. Therefore part-time work fits into their lives most easily, and does not create unrealistic expectations and dependency on the KSS.

Table 1   Staffing of the *Kantha Sahayaka Sewaya* (KSS)

	1991	1992	1993	1994
Number of KSS staff	10	7	9	7 full-time; 18 associate

Staff for the KSS are recruited in a co-operative manner: existing members identify potential recruits from their contacts with local groups. When a particular skill is required members work to identify a person. Beyond skills, the qualities of honesty and the ability to work co-operatively are emphasized. The absence of strong political allegiances is also deemed important.

The organizational structure of the credit union has developed over a five-year period. It has been a gradual process. In late 1994, primary branch leaders began to join together to form a Zonal-level to enable learning and sharing of experiences to take place between branches. The KSS has functioned as the main facilitator for this. However, it is evident that even the KSS will in future find it necessary to decentralize its support services further as the credit union grows. The Zonal-level provides a structure for this decentralization to take place.

In 1992, the groups began the process of forming primary branches and by 1994

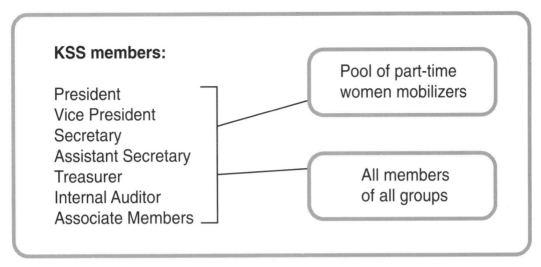

KSS members:

President
Vice President
Secretary
Assistant Secretary
Treasurer
Internal Auditor
Associate Members

Pool of part-time
women mobilizers

All members
of all groups

Figure 2   *The KSS structure*

eighteen had formed. Primary branches are the structural representation of group federation. The basic requirement is that a minimum of five groups must agree to join together to form a primary branch. The primary branch services and monitors the work of the groups. They are essentially mini-banks which function on profit–loss and are managed by the treasurers from each group.

Primary branches of the credit union work towards financial viability. They do this by pooling the resources of member groups and circulating it among these groups. Financial viability of primary branches depends on careful and accurate circulation of funds. The treasurers who manage the primary branches have gained practical experience of circulating funds at the group level before they manage a primary branch. Their skills are built up over time. Most commonly, a treasurer first manages her group's funds for a minimum of five months, then when her group joins into a primary branch she helps to manage the larger and more complex system.

Viable primary branches ensure a decentralized system of savings and credit which functions close to the members. The branch of the credit union is solvent from the initial stages because accumulated savings equal, or exceed accumulated borrowing. The groups of primary branches are, essentially, risking the loss of their own savings if they default on loan repayments.

Primary branches normally contain five groups. If the number of groups grows too large and cumbersome, some then break away and form a new primary branch. This is done most often on a geographical basis so primary branches are always composed of groups of members who live close together.

All funds, except the group's compulsory and voluntary savings, are managed at the primary branch level. Groups deposit their savings and purchase shares from their branch. They also apply to their primary branch for lending capital seven days in advance of their requirements. If approved, the lending capital is issued to the group after individuals have completed their previous loan repayments. A group is never issued overlapping or simultaneous loans from the primary branch, just as no individual borrower can take two loans at the same time.

The primary branch reviews the following records to ensure all systems have been functioning smoothly before lending money to a group:

○ share capital of the group and individuals is adequate (1:10 ratio of shares to capital must be maintained at all times);
○ the welfare funds and compulsory savings have been made on time, and to the correct amount;
○ attendance at meetings of the group and branch level have been 100%;
○ past loans have been used for the agreed purpose.

In addition to providing capital for loans to groups, the primary branch undertakes the following functions:

○ balancing the overall cash requirements of their primary branch, borrowing from the KSS/PSS when required, and monitoring cash flow;
○ functioning as a repository for the following savings funds (see also section 3.2d):
    1. compulsory individual savings of Rs.5 per month
    2. common welfare funds
    3. compulsory loan deductions
    4. group welfare funds
    5. voluntary savings
    6. fixed term deposits
    7. children's savings deposits
    8. non-member savings
○ carrying out internal auditing of group and branch financial transactions;
○ monitoring the cost of the primary branch and group operations by managing the interest paid on loans;
○ functioning as a representative, or neutral adviser, to the group: a primary branch member attends the group meeting at which in-depth discussions about loan-use take place (this is done only in cases where the amount to be borrowed exceeds Rs.2000.)

c. The parent organization: the PSS

The KSS is a small organization existing under the umbrella of its 'parent', the PSS (*Praja Sahayaka Sewaya*: Community Assistance Service). The PSS was formed during the years from 1986 to 1991 (details in Appendix 4). It is a poor people's non-governmental organization (NGO) in which all members are from low-income areas in Colombo and selected rural locations. The PSS provides an umbrella under which various activities, from housing co-operatives to the production of a local newspaper, are undertaken. Together these various initiatives have the potential to form a poor people's movement.

The PSS differs from many local NGOs in that its primary purpose is to support the growth of other community-based organizations and initiatives. It does this through raising awareness of problems and working with local people to search and implement solutions. The PSS and KSS do not take a time-bound 'project' approach to development like many NGOs. They are part of the fabric of low-income areas, woven into communities as resident activists.

Similarly to many local NGOs the PSS directs its efforts to micro-development initiatives which require an intimate understanding of and relationship with local people. They are adaptable, flexible and most of all community focused. Unlike many NGOs, however, they have the ability to bring a multitude of micro-initiatives together into the first stages of a 'movement'. An illustration of this is the women's credit union Annual General Meeting. This is a rare event in which thousands of poor women gather and speak publicly about issues which concern them. It is a dynamic and moving event which includes drama and dance produced by members to reflect their lives and situations (see section 4.1).

d. Savings

Savings by individual group members form the core capital of the women's credit union. The obligatory nature of savings is one of the key factors which ensures this credit union is owned and controlled by the poor themselves.

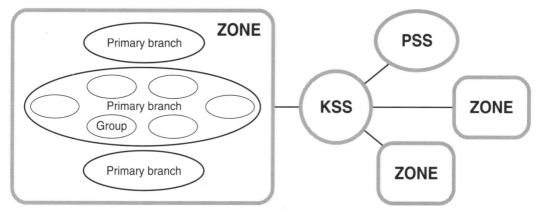

Figure 3 *The structure of the credit union and support systems (KSS and PSS)*

Low-income people have the capacity to save and often do so through informal channels that never enter the formal financial structures. Through building on this informal propensity to save, the credit union has become a valuable and empowering tool for low-income women. It contributes to an improvement in the quality of their lives. Not only does saving offer a reprieve to the constant worry that accompanies a subsistence life, it also serves to fund whatever productive activity sustains the family.

How is saving encouraged and promoted? One mechanism is through a small promotional pamphlet which is used to stimulate discussion at the group level. It was devised by KSS and PSS members. The pamphlet compares what a poor woman can save and what her husband spends on cigarettes! (see Figure 4). This is a practical tool which helps women to understand how savings can substantially accumulate over time even when only a small amount is regularly deposited.

CAN THE POOR SAVE?

How can we save? The money we earn is not enough! Shall we discuss this question by looking at an example?

Soma lives in a low-income area in Colombo. She is a group member and saves Rs.5 each week. This amount is small but it accumulates!

Let's see how this money grows with a collective approach. Soma's group has ten members. 100 groups like hers save in a year as follows:

Soma's weekly savings:	Rs.5
Soma's yearly savings:	Rs.260
Savings of 100 groups of 10 women each:	Rs.260,000

Rs.260,000 = is this a small amount?

Soma's husband, Siripala, smokes about five cigarettes in a day which costs him about Rs.12/50. He has no habit of saving.

Siripala's daily smoking expenses:	Rs.12/50
Siripala's yearly smoking expenses:	Rs.4,562/50
1000 men like Siripala:	Rs.4,562,500/

Do poor people have money to save? What do we think now?

Figure 4 *Group discussion materials, translated from Sinhala*

15

Women in this credit union prefer the discipline and routine of weekly deposits of savings. They find this easier than trying to save by themselves at home.

Various types of savings are promoted within the credit union. Some are compulsory, others are voluntary. They have been developed over a four-year period and are introduced gradually to each group. The following is a brief description of each.

Compulsory savings

Annual interest of 15% is paid on the deposits of the following compulsory savings. Compulsory savings are used as the capital which is issued as loans to members.

○ **Regular compulsory savings (individual)**
Weekly deposits by each member of Rs.5 (10 US cents). This is managed by the group as their emergency fund. The use of the emergency fund is determined by each group but normally includes loans for medicine and unexpected household needs.

○ **Compulsory savings (group)**
Rs.5 per month per member. This is managed by the primary branch.

○ **Common welfare fund**
Rs.10 per month per person (from this death donations are issued). It is non-refundable, and managed at the primary branch level.

○ **Compulsory loan deduction**
5% deduction from each individual loan of over Rs.500. This is taken at the time of issuing loans and is managed by the primary branch.

○ **Shares**
Rs.100 is the cost of each share. It is mandatory that each member own one share for every Rs.1000 she borrows. Thus, for example, each woman must have purchased two shares before she can borrow Rs.1500.

Voluntary savings

Annual interest of 12.5% per year is paid on the following savings deposits.

○ **Ad hoc voluntary savings**
Any member may save additional money at the group level if she wishes. For this interest is not paid.

○ **Fixed term deposits**
Savings deposits may be made by any individual, whether or not they are members of the women's credit union. Interest of 15.5% is paid on deposits of six months and one year. Every subsequent six month period earns interest payments of an additional 0.5%, up to a maximum of 18%.

○ **Children's savings**
Any amount may be saved by any woman or her child. There is no upper age limit on children's savings, although it generally ends before marriage.

e. Loans

Members of groups save together and borrow together. This minimizes complexities in book-keeping and reduces the likelihood of marginalization of any individual member.

Members' first loans are small. They build up to larger loans gradually and systematically over a minimum period of 18 months. This approach has been essential to the successful establishment of this credit union. It enables women to build their confidence through the experience of managing small loans. It also provides them with the means to build their businesses gradually.

At the first loan stage women borrow small amounts from their group's emergency funds. As they gain experience with this they become eligible for larger loans through their primary branch. The system has the built-in incentive of offering increasing loans as well as ensuring repayment through its inter-guarantee system between borrowers. If any group fails to repay the primary branch at any stage all members fail to be eligible for larger loans. The loan sizes are shown in Table 2.

Each woman progresses through the loan stages with her group. At any given time all group members have the same loan size and payments due. Only at Stage 4 does this pattern alter. Then only some women within a group gain access to larger housing, income-generating or ceremonial loans while the

Table 2 Loan sizes

Loan stage	Rp.	US$ equivalent
1 Emergency loans	100 (maximum)	2
2 Small monthly loans	250–500	5–10
3 Medium size loans	1000–2000	20–40
4 Larger loans	2000 and over	40

others wait their turn. Turns are decided internally by the group, most commonly on the basis of urgency of need.

Loan repayments are made by individual women to the group every week at the same time and place. Each month groups repay their loan to the primary branch. They are then issued new capital from the primary branch for the next round of loans.

Table 4 outlines the repayment system and charges.

Fines for late repayment
Groups rarely falter on repayment during Stages 1 and 2. This illustrates that small and frequent repayments are comparatively easy to manage. This is not to say that women should not be given the opportunity for larger loans; what it does illustrate, however, is that *increased loan size and longer repayment schedules must be introduced in a gradual and well planned manner which emphasize a pace which the borrowers can manage.*

The women's credit union would be pleased if no group fines were ever levied. However, when loans from the primary branch are not repaid on time the branch is compelled to fine group members.

The fine structure is as follows:
○ Delay of 1 day: 1% additional interest is charged.
○ Delay of more than 14 days: 2 weeks' interest on outstanding balance is charged.
○ Delay of more than 14 days an additional 1 month of interest is charged.

Table 3 Details of loan stages

Stage	Time frame (months)	Maximum loan size (per member) $1 = Rs.50	Description
1	5 month minimum	Rs.100 maximum	Issued by the group from accumulated savings Loans for emergencies and small production
2	5 month minimum	Rs.250 Rs.375 Rs.500 Rs.500 Rs.500	Loans for small-scale productive activities Loans for consumption
3	18 month maximum	Rs.1,000 Rs.1,500 Rs.2,000	Loans for small-scale productive activities Loans for consumption
4	Negotiable	Rs.2,000 Rs.10,000 Rs.15,000	Consumption loans up to a maximum of Rs.2,000 Income generating loans up to Rs.10,000 Housing loans up to Rs.15,000 Ceremonial loans of Rs.5,000–10,000

Issuing loans in a women's group

Table 4   Repayment system

Loan size ($1=Rs.50)	Repayment period	Service charge	System of repayment
100	Group decides	Group decides	Member repays group
250–500	1 month	4% per month	Member repays group then group repays branch
1,000–2,000	2–4 months	4% per month	Member repays group then group repays branch
2,000	2–4 months	4% per month	Members repay their group who repay the branch who repay the KSS
10,000	Minimum of Rs.250 to be repaid per month	2.5% per month	
15,000		2% per month	
5,000–10,000		4 % per month	

If a group is fined twice during any stage of borrowing, the group is down-graded to the previous loan size. This is because two delays in repayment indicates that borrowers are unable to bear the burden of repaying such large loans.

When instalment payments from the individual to the group are late the individual is fined. These fines are collected by the group then distributed among the members at the end of the year.

f. Interest rates

Interest paid on money borrowed is referred to as a 'service charge' because it is

18

Mat-weaving, a traditional income-earning activity done by many low-income Sri Lankans

considered a simpler and clearer concept for borrowers.

The interest charged to borrowers is 2% per month. This is higher than that offered by banks (average: 21% per annum, 1994). However, banks in Sri Lanka are generally inaccessible to the poor due to their requirements for collateral, references and complex form-filling. The charges levied by moneylenders, the most common source of finance for the poor in Sri Lanka, range widely but are approximately 240% per year.

Interest rates on loans
○ The interest charged on loans from the group to the individual: 4% per month (48% per year).
○ The interest charged on loans made from the branch to the group level: 4% a month.
○ The interest charged on loans made from the KSS to the branch: 1.25% a month.

Interest charged on loans is used in several ways: to cover the costs of work done by group leaders, to build up the welfare funds, and to pay interest on savings.

The interest paid on savings deposits has always been considerably higher than the average of 12.5% paid by mainstream formal banks.

Interest rates paid on savings (annual)
○ Interest paid on savings at the primary branch: 12.5%
○ Interest paid on children's savings: 15%
○ Interest paid on compulsory savings: 15%
○ Interest paid on fixed deposits: 15.5% and upwards

Interest is not paid on savings kept at the group level which is used as emergency funds for lending to groups members (see compulsory savings, section 3.2d).

19

3.3 A Step-by-Step Approach to Group Formation

Social mobilizing is a fundamental part of the KSS's work in supporting this credit union. It is through mobilizing that women break their individual isolation and are able to gain strength and confidence through groups. Mobilizing is done by experienced women members. It serves to spread information about the union's purpose and functions.

How does this mobilizing happen? And how are groups formed and supported? The process is both ad hoc and systematic. News of events and changes within low-income settlements spreads quickly! Women talk about what they are doing to their neighbours, in the market, and at almost any meeting point including health clinics, water points, on the bus and as they travel on the train. As a result, the general idea of the women's credit union spreads quickly. Many women contact the KSS in search of more detailed information and for support and advice. The 'systematic' approach then begins. This is described in the step-by-step process outlined below.

Women are free to decide who to join with to form a group. The better-off women in low-income areas seldom join because of the length of time required in saving before receiving a loan (Stage 1) and the comparatively small size of the loans. In Sri Lanka's highly stratified social structure the better-off do not seek access to these loans, as explained by the KSS: *'The better-off are not patient enough to come together, save and eventually after a minimum of five months, receive a small loan.'*

Groups do sometimes contain men if the women members request it. In Colombo's urban groups, there are no male group members. In the rural groups there are a handful. This is most common in cases of extreme poverty in which the men are widowers with young children. In such cases, the decision to include them is taken locally. However, the office-bearing posts are never held by men. In cases such as in the area of *Kalutara* in which there are three men, the men participate quietly and are considered by the women to be a very positive element.

The women's credit union is growing and it is the responsibility of the KSS to support and promote this growth. They do this by facilitating and supporting the formation of new groups through the following step-by-step process.

Step 1: Sharing experiences and information

Requests often come to the KSS from informal groupings of women who want to know more about the savings and credit activities. These meetings, and all subsequent group meetings, are held in a designated member's house at a specific time. This initial work is done by a pool of part-time women mobilizers who have practical experience from forming their own group and are committed to working to expand the credit union. During this initial meeting the ideas and basic systems are explained. These include:

○ the purpose of the Women's Credit Union;
○ the functions of the group;
○ the manner and procedure of meetings;
○ the way in which they should choose their leader;
○ discussion of social development activities.

Initial contact contains both practical information and discussion about the wider concepts of why such a credit union has come into existence. It is the beginning of a process of broadening poor women's understanding of societal issues and the power gained through unity. It is also a time of building poor women's self-confidence, inner strength and dignity. It is a dynamic time, when the poor support others to join their own development process.

There are very few groups which 'drop out' of the formation process, but those who have illustrate the importance of KSS support during the initial stages of formation. Without support, starting a savings group is very difficult. Groups require a clear sense of purpose and direction. They also find strength from understanding and being part of the larger credit union, rather than an isolated group. Support which is both consistent and regular is vital to group development.

Is this initial step always reactive, rather than pro-active? During the early development of the credit union in urban Colombo (1991–92) the KSS worked pro-actively: going to women in low-income areas and discussing the system. In an effort to involve rural women a pro-active approach has also been taken by KSS members. They visit rural villages and explain about the credit union and their own work. The village members are given time to decide if they wish to pursue the formation of a local branch of the credit union. This often involves a visit to a primary branch in another location to have informal discussions with women who have taken the step to join. Participation is, therefore, open and voluntary. This contrasts with many development initiatives in Sri Lanka in which the poor are influenced into participating by political alliances and material incentives.

During the years 1992–94 the KSS functioned more reactively than pro-actively. New groups were supported on request and there was a limited amount of decision-taking by the KSS as to where or when this might happen in any given area. By mid-1994, it was becoming clear that there was a need to become pro-active once again. This resulted from the realization that the KSS's strength as an urban initiative was being increasingly drawn to rural areas where, in some instances, alternative credit systems existed or were being developed. At

the same time many urban areas had little access to reasonably priced credit. Thus discussions to broaden the base of the number of urban groups was being considered at the time of writing this document.

Step 2: Deciding to participate

Women take time to decide whether to participate in forming a group and joining the process. This is an important step in building trust between themselves and towards the wider membership.

Experience has shown that women frequently require six to eight weeks minimum to decide whether or not to participate. Pressures of funding and reporting deadlines which so often force the pace of development projects are not factors which determine the pace of growth for this credit union. Experience has illustrated that it is important to give women adequate time to form groups in which there is trust among members.

There may be from five to fifteen members in any group. Members of a group need not be producing or selling the same type of product, however, they must live in close proximity to each other and trust each other.

New groups are guided by members from well established groups, thus they are able to begin shaping themselves according to the qualities and values of other groups who have already made the difficult journey of becoming established. The guiding member may be a KSS staff person or a part-time woman mobilizer from another group. They impress on the new group members that they are partners in a well planned, systematic and disciplined movement. The history of the movement is explained to new members, plus the vital ingredients of:

○ collective strength;
○ collective responsibility;
○ openness, frankness, and discipline.

It is at this point that new groups are exposed to rules. The first rules they are given

21

are very basic and set the foundation for the more detailed rules they are required to learn in Step 4.

Basic group rules

1. Those attending group meetings should only be poor women.
2. Members must live in the same neighbourhood.
3. Only one member from each family should be in any group.
4. Only persons who can trust each other in money transactions should be members of a group.
5. No moneylenders or loan sharks should join a group.
6. Leaders of any group should **NOT**:
    ○ be actively involved in politics;
    ○ be office-bearers in community development or other associations;
    ○ be functioning in other development support teams (such as the *Praja Sahayaka Sewaya* or *Janasaviya*).

These rules are carefully adhered to in most instances but, as illustrated above (paragraph 4, section 3.3), even the stipulation that all members must be women is sometimes waived in the face of extreme adversity. This may be seen by observers as a weakness in the system, but it also serves to illustrate the differences which emerge when poor people are given the power to take decisions.

'Poor' is, in the case of the PSS and KSS, defined primarily by residence. If you live in the 'slum' or 'shanty' you qualify to become a member. However, it is clear that those who are better-off do not choose to join this credit union (see paragraph 3, section 3.3).

Step 3: Getting equipped

Once the decision to join the credit union has been made, the group decides the time and place for its regular weekly meeting. The meetings are always held on the same day and in the same location, often in the home of the group's selected chairperson or treasurer. A meeting lasts from 15 to 45 minutes, depending on the business and issues to be discussed.

Each group selects its own Chairperson, Secretary and Treasurer. Their responsibilities are:

○ Chairperson: to call and conduct all meetings;
○ Secretary: to record all meeting minutes;
○ Treasurer: to do all monetary transactions, keep accounts and keep the money box.

New groups receive various tools to begin their work. These are supplied by the KSS and include:

○ a small steel box and key;
○ a pencil and eraser;
○ a ruler and a file;
○ 3 ledgers (CR1 books);
○ a red-ink pen, two blue ink pens.

They are taught the pattern of recording meeting minutes and keeping records of attendance.

It is at this stage that the members also begin to save. Savings are recorded in the ledger and individual passbooks. This allows the new Treasurer, as well as each individual member, to know exactly how much has been saved.

Getting used to the book-keeping system is enhanced by starting the system of group emergency loans. Funds for lending are from the group's accumulated savings. A maximum of Rs.100 can be borrowed by any group member as long as she has the other members' consent. It is through this experience that the members gain more confidence in the group methodology, lending and repaying and group solidarity.

Step 4: The test

As the members save and become accustomed to the routine and discipline, they also learn the more detailed rules of the system. In this way their general knowledge is

Low-income Sri Lankan women are extremely capable; this is Mrs Rupa Manel, a group leader, a member of the KSS, a wife, a mother and a business woman

built up over time and in increasing detail. The details of these rules are outlined on the following page.

A printed copy of the rules is given to each woman. If she is illiterate she is helped by other group members or a person from her family. Each woman must memorize and understand all the rules. The test of her understanding is done verbally by a person from another established group. Each new group member is asked five questions in the presence of the other group members. Every member must pass this test, and through this process the group becomes eligible for formal membership to the Women's Credit Union.

Step 5: The milestones of becoming a formal credit union member

---

Having successfully completed the previous steps, the new group may now become a member of the women's credit union. This is an important milestone as it represents solidarity and association with other groups and the point when they are part of the formal credit union movement. New groups, during their pre-cooperative stage, are at least five months old by the time they reach this stage. While each member joins the union individually, it is at this point that they open a group bank account. By this stage the group becomes eligible for borrowing lending capital from the primary branch of the credit union.

Each individual must contribute Rs.125 to join the credit union. This is composed of:

○ Rs.100 = one share in the union
○ Rs.10 = membership fee
○ Rs.10 = monthly welfare fund contribution
○ Rs.5   = monthly savings contribution

The group then is guided in the production of a seal and stamp for their group. This is

Detailed group rules for savings and credit

1. Group membership can only be held by residents of the same neighbourhood.
2. The total group size should not be fewer than five or more than fifteen.
3. All members must attend the weekly meeting of their group, set on a specific day and time.
4. All group members must save Rs.5 per week.
5. Only one woman from any family may participate in a group. She must be 18 years old or older.
6. The chairperson, secretary and treasurer of each group should be selected by the group members. The treasurer should be the leader of the group.
7. Records of finance should be kept by the treasurer. Records of meeting minutes and attendance should be kept by the secretary. The conducting of meetings should be done by the chairperson.
8. The group's leaders should not be involved in politics or moneylending. In the event that a moneylender is found in a group, the group will remove her and she shall not receive any payments of benefits.
9. Emergency loans of Rs.100 (US$2) may be issued to members from their savings held at the group level. These should be repaid within a week and with a service charge of Rs.1.
10. The cash box should be kept by the treasurer. The key to the cash box should be kept by another group member as decided by the group.
11. The cash box and key must be brought to each group's weekly meeting.
12. After a group has functioned smoothly for five months and has passed the test on these rules, they are eligible to become members of the Poor Women's Credit and Savings Union.
13. Every group, once they have joined the union, should open an account with the Colombo District Women's Thrift and Credit Co-operative Society.
14. A group which has satisfactorily completed the steps outlined above may be eligible to borrow lending capital from their primary branch for onward lending to group members.
15. The lending capital mentioned above is issued as a loan from the Colombo District Women's Thrift and Credit Co-operative Society and is primarily the accumulated savings of the groups.
16. Loans to members must be made in the following stages:
    Stage 1: Loan size, Rs.250 (US$5), repayable in four weekly instalments with a service charge of 1% a week.

weekly payment:	Rs.62/50
weekly savings:	Rs.5
weekly service charge:	Rs.2/50
Total:	Rs. 70

17. After successfully completing Stage 1, a second loan of Rs.375 may be taken by each member:

weekly payment:	Rs.93/75
weekly savings:	Rs.5
weekly service charge:	Rs.3/75
Total:	Rs.102/50

18. After successfully completing Stage 2, a third loan of Rs.500 may be taken by each member.

weekly payment:	Rs.125
weekly savings:	Rs.5
weekly service charge:	Rs.5
Total:	Rs.135

19. After transacting loans of Rs.500 for three cycles a group may be considered competent and may become eligible for graduating to further loan stages.
20. If any member of a group defaults from repaying their loan, the remaining members will take responsibility for making her payment. The group will decide on the defaulter's status within the group.
21. Individual group members should not intermingle their personal transactions with those of the groups.
22. All members should work in the spirit of co-operation and avoid conflict within their group or towards other groups.
23. Any designated member of the credit union should be allowed access to records kept by any group for perusal and auditing purposes.

considered an important indication of the group's legal recognition and official status in the context of Sri Lanka.

Step 6: Membership books

Once membership to the credit union is fully agreed, the membership books are issued. By this stage the foundation to manage the growing complexity of the union has been well established.

The individual group member is issued with a Member's Passbook:

THE MEMBER'S YELLOW PASSBOOK

This is the individual's record of all her transactions within the credit union. It records all her savings, the shares she has purchased, the loans and repayments she has made as well as the interest paid during each transaction. It is signed by the Treasurer of the primary branch and herself every time money changes hands. Thus the book acts as the member's account as well as her receipt.

At the group level, two books are kept:

THE MEMBERS' WHITE PASSBOOK

This is the overall record of transaction within the group. It records group savings and loans, as well as each person's repayments. It provides an 'overview' of how the group is progressing.

THE GROUP PASSBOOK

The group opens an account in the primary branch. This passbook records the money the group has borrowed from the primary branch, and the interest charges. This also records the group welfare funds.

Step 7: On-going functions

There is much to be said in favour of the repetition required to run a group or primary branch within this credit union. Perhaps most importantly is the fact that repetition builds all the members' capacity to manage finance on both a personal and group level. In a practical sense, the on-going group functions include:

○ meeting weekly to make savings and collect loan repayments;
○ negotiating among themselves the use of their group emergency fund: its use as lending capital, and its use in the instance of an individual not able to repay her loan instalment on time;
○ social development issues and ideas (see Chapter 4).

3.4 When Things Go Wrong

No credit and savings operation is trouble-free, and there have been cases in this women's credit union, like all others, when money has gone missing, has not been repaid, or has had to be rescheduled. Although these are infrequent occurrences, the following cases illustrate the problems which have arisen and how they were resolved with the assistance of the KSS and PSS. They are described by the KSS members, who explained, *'We are not afraid of mistakes, but we are afraid of repeating them!'*

Case 1: Personal emergencies

The first case of money being stolen occurred in 1990 during the pilot phase of development. One of the groups had been issued Rs.3500 for their revolving fund, and they had savings in their cash box. The group was managing the savings and lending transactions, but one day a group member went to the KSS and said, *'We don't have money in our box for emergency loans. The group leader told me to come and tell you.'* The PSS member replied, *'I have nothing to do with emergency loans given by your group, and anyway you MUST have money in the cash box.'* The same week the

The Kantha Sahayaka Sewaya (KSS) at work

members met with the PSS, and checked the records and the cash box. There was no money in the box, although the written records showed there should have been. The leader admitted taking the money for her ill child and her husband's medical expenses. The group wanted to continue the lending system: they revised the leadership. The old leader was still allowed to be a member but not to hold an office bearer's position. The group began borrowing again but the woman's situation meant she was not a reliable borrower and it became obvious that she was holding back her group's progress. She repaid very small amounts very slowly, and eventually she was asked to leave the first group and join a new group which was at the first loan stage. The new group is fully aware of her previous difficulties. She realizes her fault, and others sympathize with her difficult circumstances.

As a result of this first case, the overall system for the use of the cash box at the group level was revised. Now no single person is allowed to keep both the box and the key. Therefore, to remove any money without the group's approval requires a conspiracy of more than one member.

Case 2: The stolen box

In a very poor section of Colombo near the Kelani River where people live in homes made of straw, the group leader left to take her son to school. When she returned she discovered the cash box was missing. It had been kept in a glass cupboard. Luckily it only contained a small amount of money (Rs.850) from the accumulated savings of the group. The leader went immediately to the KSS office and explained. Then she went to the police station. She suspected a particular man and the police took action and arrested him. The suspect's wife came to the house of the group leader and threatened her, and so she withdrew her suspicions against the man. She came to the KSS office and they issued a new box with Rs.1000 loan. The money was given to cover the costs which she had to bear in getting to the KSS and to the police to report the incident. Nonetheless, the group leader had to repay the stolen money monthly at 1% interest. It took her 10 months.

Case 3: The key holder

In the credit group which is called *Kumari*, the cash box is kept by the group's Treasurer. Her husband is a heroin addict. She used to go to the other group member who kept the cash box key and request it from time to time. The keeper of the key gave it to her without questioning. The key holder was not an active woman and she was known for frequently giving the key to other group members too so that they could withdraw money themselves by going to the Treasurer.

The general rule for all groups is that every week at the group meeting the cash box has to be opened and the money counted, but this group did not do this regularly. They failed to follow this rule and some of the money disappeared in late 1993 (about Rs.4000). The Treasurer had taken the money, but it was nearly six months before the other group members realized the problem. It was only then that she admitted taking the money.

The group members met with the KSS and discussed the problem. The reliable members formed a new group which excluded the Treasurer as well as her mother and her mother's elder sister from the group. The members of the new group took the responsibility of re-collecting the outstanding money, and the Treasurer's father agreed to repay the money. By October 1994, Rs.3000 had been repaid to the newly formed group.

Case 4: The conspiracy not to pay

In a particular group of ten members there was a conspiracy not to repay the loan. They

had been functioning very well for more than one year and had reached the stage where each member was eligible for a loan of Rs.1000. On the last day of the repayment of the Rs.1000 loans the group leader and one member decided to accept the next loan (Rs.1500) and not to pay any of it. They asked the others, *'shall we take the money and not pay it back?'*. The group kept quiet. A few members then went to the KSS the next day. By this time the application for supplementary funds had been submitted to the primary branch requesting money for larger loans. *'We don't like this conspiracy and want to continue. Please stop the loan. We want to reform the group without these two members.'* The loans were stopped and no capital was given to the group by the primary branch. The KSS did not go to the group, the women solved the problem themselves by reforming the group. The reformed group applied for funds from the branch. It included only the trustworthy members. The KSS then agreed that the group should be allowed to borrow Rs.1000 each again.

They are now functioning very well, and have indeed purchased two sewing machines on credit from the PSS.

Case 5: A group collapse

One well established group collapsed at the final loan stage in which each member could borrow Rs.2000. Two members of this group of eleven did not repay any of their Rs.2000 loan. The problem was rooted in a disagreement over leadership: some group members felt the leader was unable to keep the accounts and meeting minutes adequately. One member who was especially cunning wanted the leadership. She frequently went to the KSS office to complain about the existing leader, saying the leader could not manage the group well. The KSS investigated and found that the leader actually wanted to learn and was highly motivated, but the cunning woman held power and influence over others in the community. The leader felt reluctant and intimidated. When the group reached the stage where they had access to the largest loans, only nine members repaid their loans in full. The group eventually collapsed, but without finance being lost at the primary branch level because the group's accumulated savings and shares exceeded the balance of the outstanding loan instalments to be paid.

Case 6: Natural disaster tips the financial balance at branch level

Groups sometimes use their emergency funds to repay loan instalments due to the primary branch. This happens when an individual member faces extreme personal difficulties. When this happens the group bears the burden by taking some of their accumulated Group Emergency Funds and paying the primary branch. The individual then has to repay the Group Emergency Fund as well as the next instalment due to the primary branch. Thus the Group Emergency Fund is sometimes used to cover delays in loan repayments and serves to safeguard the solvency of the primary branch.

This system has only broken down once: when a major flood occurred in Colombo in June 1992. Rains had been heavy for several days and the canals overflowed and washed away hundreds of people's houses. The city was in chaos, including the PSS/KSS office, based in the middle of the largest low-income area in Colombo. The office is situated on high ground, and many residents settled in to wait for the water to subside. In addition to these flood refugees, three women's credit union groups of approximately 30 women in total came to request that they be allowed to pay only the service charge on their loans for the month because their lives were in chaos due to the floods.

Although this emergency situation tipped the balance of finance at several primary branches, it was a temporary problem which was overcome with short-term financing from the PSS and international donors. Because it is exceptional the women's credit union does not feel that such circumstances put into question the fundamental viability of their system.

4

More than Money: Social development and housing activities

Social Development Activities supplement the savings and credit functions of the Women's Credit Union. The banking functions of the credit union are perceived as the 'entry point' of work and are followed by broader-based social development activities. These include the Children's Cultural Programme which puts particular emphasis on the daughters of the Women's Credit Union members. Assistance through the provision of glasses for the elderly, a school book scheme, a death donation scheme, and pilot housing loans are all important parts of the credit union work in low-income areas. The following provides an overview of how low-income people have developed and manage these activities.

4.1 The Children's Cultural Programme

The Children's Cultural Programme grew out of the Women's Credit Union in 1993. There are three key objectives which illustrate the changing role of the performing arts in the lives of low-income people.

The first objective is to *promote cultural activities among children of low-income areas*, especially for those who have no access to creative learning. Barriers to this exist because low-income parents often do not feel that cultural studies such as dancing and music are of any particular benefit to their children's futures. Parents neglect these activities because they frequently consider the arts as unrelated to their children's future ability to earn an income.

The second programme objective is to *use cultural media as a means of presenting the key issues of low-income urban family life*. Drama and music are used to express concerns about housing, land, sanitation, and income generation. Historically in Sri Lanka songs, drama and poems were aesthetic means of expression of the interests and concerns of people. The Cultural Programme seeks to revitalize this tradition.

The final objective is to *protect and promote the indigenous cultural heritage of the performing arts* in Sri Lanka. This is done through teaching children traditional skills such as the four types of traditional dancing: low country, up country, *sabaragamuwa* (from Ratnapura area), and *Bharatha Natyam* (from India).

The Children's Cultural Programme works through groups. Cultural groups, called *Sangka* (meaning conch shell[8]), are formed by the children of members of the Women's Credit Union. Mothers encourage their children to join, thus forming a link between the Credit Union and child development.

By 1994, ten groups had formed involving approximately 200 children from age nine upwards to marriage. More than 75% of those involved are girls who in future may become part of the Women's Credit Union.

Dancing, drama and music (singing and instrumental) are taught weekly by teachers hired from funds from the PSS. The instructors are generally not from low-income families, as these skills have been dying among low-income people over recent generations. The PSS plans, through this programme, to revitalize the performing arts among low-income people. They provide practical support to the teachers through the provision of some musical instruments. Traditional songs

Children ready for a performance

are learned and new songs are composed by the children. Dramatic techniques are also taught.

The groups meet to learn and perform each month. There is a one-day drama training workshop held within a community centre in one low-income area known as *Bandaranaikapura.* All the children are welcome to attend. In addition, the children perform at the Annual General Meeting of the Women's Credit Union.

In several groups the children have decided to save money in order to buy musical instruments. They do this by contributing Rs.1 each per week to an account they have opened in their mothers' credit union primary branch. If the children do not have enough money for what they need they sometimes take loans from their mothers' group. These loans are interest free; the capital comes from the PSS, but is managed by the mothers' credit union primary branch. To date three loans have helped to purchase drums and an Indian accordion (*serpinya*).

Children's creativity is released and enhanced through this programme which helps to build their confidence. In addition, parents learn of their children's creative potential: *'Their songs are like those we hear on the radio and television,'* explained one parent. Lyrics to songs are written by children in the Cultural Programme. They write these as a group, not as individuals, because this encourages them to work co-operatively. Although adult artists often complain about their own lack of creative inspiration, these children's groups never complain about not having ideas or not being in the mood for creating songs and poems!

Local drama performances are prepared and performed regularly by children in the

30

Cultural Programme. The topics relate to their social life and folk stories. The folk stories are adapted to relate to the lives of common poor people. This is done by the children themselves who prepare the dialogue and songs, and then perform these for all who live in their area.

Traditional dance techniques are taught step by step. Some children have progressed into a more advanced class and are well on the way to becoming instructors.

4.2 Housing Loans

For people from low-income urban areas of Colombo, gaining access to land, common amenities and housing is often their first major collective priority. As described earlier, this mobilization was encouraged by a government programme for shelter improvement which included the early development of the Women's Credit Union. Indeed, mobilization for housing has proven to be a successful foundation from which community members gain experience in organizing, articulating their needs, identifying resources and managing the development process. Though many more men gained these skills than women during the 1980s and early 1990s, the process enabled a number of low-income community leaders to emerge.

In areas where land rights and upgrading of common amenities has taken place there is strong motivation and interest among women to form groups for savings and credit. They give several reasons for this:

○ the design of their house is often linked to the growth of their home-based business (see below);
○ women often feel that an upgraded house helps make a successful business;
○ women believe it is easier to save in a group than to save individually at home;
○ housing builds up the family's capital resources and wealth-base.

In areas which have benefited from housing and amenity improvements, businesses such as small shops and tailors multiply visibly where they seemed previously to have barely existed. Less visible home-based producers, most of whom are women making food and consumables, also increase. The need for production space clearly and directly affects the design of these people's homes. Some of the more common design alterations are outlined in the box overleaf.

Members of the Women's Credit Union are determined to emphasize the link between improved housing areas and successful businesses. In these areas families devote an increased amount of time to their enterprise once the new home is completed. An upgraded home also has implications for business success. One women's leader explained:

Among the poor there are standards. People with upgraded and clean houses have more customers and better businesses!

The Women's Credit Union was urged by its longstanding members to pilot a system of housing loans in 1993. The need culminated as a result of a serious flood in Colombo in June 1992. Women and their families from *Seevalipura*, the largest low-income settlement area in Colombo were displaced and their houses ruined. The Women's Credit Union responded by beginning a small pilot housing-loan system on an experimental basis.

Initially ten loans were given to women flood 'refugees' who had temporarily settled with their families in the offices of the PSS and KSS. These people were not able to access government housing loans because of the requirements of guarantors and the need for proof of earnings certificates. The KSS supported the formation of these women into two 'special' groups for housing loans.

The KSS stressed to these women the importance of their role as the first to receive housing loans. They told them that future access by other low-income people to such loans depended on their smooth repayment.

Enterprise and house design	
Type of enterprise	**Changes in house design details**
Food producers are concerned about the kitchen area:	
lunch packets	* floor space increased
breakfast foods	* area for firewood specified
catering	* ventilation improved
	* floor space for grinding stone
	* enlarged counter space
Producers of consumables are concerned about the front room and outside area:	
betel and cigars	* production area specified
joss sticks	* drying/cutting space specified
papadams	
paper bags	
Traders and small shop owners are concerned about the area facing footpaths:	
	* custom designed
	* enlarged windows for trading
	* widened footpaths
Garment producers are concerned about front or bedroom area:	
	* designed for private fittings
	* storage and production space
Tea shop owners are mainly concerned about the front room and kitchen:	
	* seating area defined
	* production area enlarged

Capital for these loans was made available from the United Nations Centre for Human Settlements (UNCHS) through the PSS. Loans of Rs.10,000 were issued first, then, dependent on the progress of their individual house construction, further loans were issued until the house was complete. The key rule which guided lending was that any individual woman's outstanding loan balance should never exceed Rs.15,000. There is no upper limit to borrowing: the outstanding balance is what controls the loan.

Only those women living in areas where they had obtained land rights (security of tenure) were eligible for housing loans; squatters were not eligible. This is the case because of the risk the loan fund would face if it provided funds to women without land tenure: the authorities retain the right to remove squatters, even if they seldom exercise this right. In such circumstances re-collection of loans would be extremely difficult.

Following the successful repayment of loans in *Seevalipura,* the housing loan system began to be extended to other members of the Women's Credit Union. Selection was done on the basis of being a member of a mature group who had managed Rs.2000 productive loans for an extended period of time. As of late 1994, five out of eighteen primary branches had issued housing loans. Approximately 50 women had gained access to these loans. The main financial management of housing loans is at the primary branch level of the credit union.

4.3 Additional Social Support

a. Failing sight

Apart from the Children's Cultural Programme and Housing Loans, the Women's Credit Union addresses other social needs such as those of the elderly. There are many low-income people suffering from poor eyesight and cataracts in Colombo and in rural areas of Sri Lanka. When they attend an eye clinic they become aware of the possibility of having an operation to correct cataracts. Following the operation they often require glasses.

The PSS and KSS provide an important network of information for the low-income people about forthcoming eye clinics. The ordering and obtaining of the glasses is done by The Lions Club and Rotary Clubs on a charitable basis. Such charities are not, however, able to organize clinics; in these instances the PSS and KSS take the initiative. They arrange a place for the doctor and inform the people. Clinics are held free of charge in low-income areas. People needing glasses are then able to purchase them on credit from the welfare fund of their Women's Union primary branch. These loans are interest free. For example, a pair of glasses may cost Rs.400. A person in need may get the glasses and repay their Women's Union primary branch a total of Rs.50 per month for eight months.

b. School books

Most Sri Lankan parents buy school books in December of each year. It usually costs on average Rs.300 per child. The Women's Union primary branch makes loans available to members of up to this maximum of Rs.300 per child. Women then repay this within ten months, interest free. Mobilizing money for school books is a heavy burden for many poor parents who place a high priority on their children's education. It is contended that the lack of funds for school books is a major contributing factor to school drop-outs.

c. Training for young women

The KSS has organized training for young women in order to build their skills for the future. One of the most promising training initiatives is in bridal dressmaking. The wedding of most young women in Sri Lanka is one of the most significant days of their lives and a large investment is made on the bridal dress. The profit margin is extremely high, and most dresses are made by middle-income dressmakers. By training women from low-income families to make these dresses, the KSS is helping young women to find a market niche for their future and retaining money in their communities.

d. Death donations

There is a long tradition of informal death donations in Sri Lanka. For married members of the Women's Credit Union funeral costs are covered by the Union in the event of her death, or her husband's, her parents, or the unmarried children's death. This is not a loan, it is a grant. This initiative helps to regularize the administration of death donations and enables access to large loans due to advantages of scale.

5

Towards Sustainability and Scaling-up

The Women's Credit Union is working towards financial sustainability at the primary branch level. On a week-by-week basis this requires continual financial balancing between repayments received from groups and loans issued to groups. These combine with the accumulated savings of each group and enable the overall capital of the primary branch to grow. Through regular and accurate balancing of finance at the branch level, ownership and control is kept close to the borrower. This is one of the strengths of a credit union approach. There are, nonetheless, key points when a primary branch requires additional capital, such as when several groups reach the stage of being eligible for relatively large housing loans. These points of capital shortage are tackled either by postponing a group's access to a primary branch loan for a short period while further repayments and savings are accumulated, or by seeking additional capital through a loan to the branch from the KSS or PSS. The KSS and PSS are the access point for international aid funding.

Loss of capital through default, both at the group and primary branch levels, is nearly non-existent in this system. This is because of a combination of factors, including:

○ the concern of individuals to retain their group's credibility and internal trust;
○ the loss of accumulated and children's savings if an individual defaults;
○ the loss of access to death benefits if an individual defaults;
○ the threat of legal action.

Financial sustainability may be feasible at the group level and the primary branch level. The question remains, however, as to whether a critical mass of borrowers can be reached to generate the required income to cover the costs of the KSS support service. This seems unlikely in the medium term. The support and development function filled by the KSS is an aspect which is likely to require external financial assistance for several years. The required level of international financial assistance is, however, modest. For the four years of 1990–94 a total budget of approximately $120,000 was needed to cover the salaries and recurrent costs of the PSS and KSS. This included the wages of 14 workers, who are on local wage rates and use local public transport for all of their fieldwork. This is extremely cost-effective when compared with international non-governmental organizations (NGO).

Towards Scaling-up

Scaling-up refers to the concept of expansion or the process of reaching ever-increasing numbers of low-income women, and of supporting their unified growth and strength. The Women's Credit Union has reached the point when decisions about how to expand and sustain themselves require detailed analysis and strategic planning. Although the Women's Credit Union system is unique in its level of participation, control and management by the poor themselves, it hangs in the balance between small-scale and expansion like so many other credit and savings initiatives throughout developing countries.

Approximately five years have been required to develop the base of the organization: the groups and the primary branch savings and loan mechanisms. The Women's Credit Union now has over 3500 members and is beginning to consolidate and look to expansion. By 1994, the number of members outside of central Colombo urban area exceeded those in Colombo's main low-income areas. Presently the Credit Union involves less than 2 per cent of the total number of low-income women in Colombo itself. Still, the issue of scaling-up needs to be put in perspective: to those who have worked to bring this credit union into existence, having 3500 members of whom more than 2000 attend their Annual General Meeting is a remarkable accomplishment for a poor people's initiative which is not led by a political party or external NGO. The KSS and PSS are now, however, beginning to challenge their own perception of scale. They are beginning to undertake further social mobilizing and expand the credit union. They wish to do this in a way which does not build a heavy and cumbersome hierarchy. Consideration is being given to ways in which to decentralize and multiply the KSS into small support units.

Many important questions which will guide their future need to be debated and discussed. Among these are overall issues of strategic priorities:

○ **Existing versus new lending mechanisms**: Should the number of types of loans and savings mechanisms be increased for the benefit of established members? Or should the mechanisms stabilize in a way which gives future emphasis to reaching new borrowers? This is not an easily re-solved issue as the strongest pressure is exerted by women who are already members and would like further benefits of larger loans. How committed will the existing members be to focusing the credit union's energies on bringing in further members? It is likely that a compromise will be reached which provides some form of new loans to existing members as well as reaching new borrowers.

○ **Rural expansion versus an urban focus**: Can the union successfully expand in both? By the end of 1994 they had reached eight urban areas and twelve rural local authorities. Within Sri Lanka there are many development organizations working on credit in rural areas but few work with the urban poor through savings and credit. The comparative strength of this credit union needs to be considered and an answer sought to the question: What is the priority focus of KSS support, rural or urban?

○ **Reactive versus pro-active expansion**: Should the KSS respond to requests from new groups, or actively mobilize individuals to form groups where they do not exist to date?

6

Conclusion

Credit unions can support the realization of poor people's aspirations. Building one is a long and complex journey, but one which can reverse the process of conventional development approaches. One of the fundamental requirements before embarking on such a journey is a clear and firm commitment to development as *'people taking control over what they need to work with'*.[9] This goes beyond the mechanistic notion of development as increasing physical assets and the flow of goods and services. People mobilizing, enquiring, deciding and taking action of their own is an end in itself and not just the means of development. If poor people are moving in this way to assert themselves, who is to say they should be 'developing' differently? The very notion of 'poverty', conventionally conceived in consumerist terms, distracts from the vital element of self-determination. Is 'development' only about living standards? The people in this credit union answer the question cautiously.

The communities whose efforts are described here may be 'poor' by material standards of the so-called 'rich', but are immensely rich themselves in culture and values. This is illustrated in the collective endeavour of the credit union. We are working towards better standards of living through credit and savings, but our development is also about our strength as a union and a voice for the poor.

The Women's Credit Union reinforces some of the old principles which the co-operative movement has advocated for over 150 years. What is important in this credit union is the innovations. These include the formation of pre-cooperative groups as a starting point and the key role of the KSS in undertaking social mobilization.

There has been, and will continue to be, a role for external persons in this process, but only in the shadows of the poor, not as decision-takers. Their role is focused on animation and facilitation and as providers of technical information.

The challenge for external organizations is to support this process in which the agenda and priorities of the credit union are set by the poor themselves. External organizations often use such initiatives to deliver and address their own priorities. This reverses the process of developing poor people's self-determination but is often an inviting 'threat' to the poor who are lured by resources and promises of partnerships which only prove to reinforce dependency.

An important message lies in the choice of a credit union mechanism as a tool for development. Credit unions are democratically owned co-operative societies and are built on membership and principles of equity. Their foundation is small pre-cooperative groups who federate together to form the 'union'. This union is not controlled or owned by non-borrowers. It challenges conventional 'banking for the poor' in which institutions are built by professionals who by and large lead a life very different from the poor borrowers who they seek to serve. The recent development trend in banking for the poor has for the most part focused on access to resources. The wider issues of power and control have been inadequately considered. If 'self-determination' and empowerment of the poor are goals, then careful consideration must be given to the type of organizational structure through which credit and savings is promoted. It is essential to address the issue of *who controls and holds power*? Structures which hold the power for, and on behalf of, the poor promote dependency rather than self-determination. This brings into question the relevance of approaches and institutional structures which promote 'banking for the poor'.[10]

The current challenge is to move beyond delivery of credit and savings, to a situation in which the poor themselves own the process as well as the mechanisms of development. It is beyond both welfarism and the free market, and requires the recognition of people's abilities to create their own organizations. This is not a new concept. Indeed it was pioneered by the Rochdale Society of Equitable Pioneers in 1844 who expressed it this way:

They took their affairs into their own hands, and what is more to the purpose, they kept them in their own hands.

Notes

1 Tilakartna, S., 1986, 'Organisation of the Poor', unpublished paper.

2 Development organizations frequently promote the use of the 'SMART' framework of analysis. This sets as priority objectives which are specific, measurable, achievable, realistic and timebound.

3 de Silva, GVS, et al., 1979.

4 Tilakaratna, S., 1987.

5 For further details on the facilitator's role, see Tilakaratna, 1987.

6 Gregario, Angelita, 1985, *'Rural Development Animators: Some Experiences from the Philippinos'*, Geneva, ILO, unpublished.

7 UNICEF: United Nations Childrens Fund, and UNCHS: United Nations Centre for Human Settlements.

8 The conch shell symbolizies purity in Sri Lankan culture.

9 Translated from the concept of 'development' from Sindebele, a local language in Matabeleland.

10 There are significant differences between the concept and implementation of the credit union described here and that of Grameen Bank and other 'banking institutions for the poor'. One fundamental difference is that there are no employed middle-class bank workers delivering, administering or deciding on who receives loans in this credit union. Although, in the instance of Grameen, they are now considering devolving some of the administrative responsibilities to group leaders, this has been necessary primarily because of their increasing costs of loan delivery. The most significant difference between co-operative and institutional approaches to credit lies in the answer to the questions: *Who takes decisions?* and *Who controls the funds?*

11 UNCHS (Habitat), *The Urban Poor as Agents of Development*, 1993, p. 11.

12 Gamage, Nandasiri, *'Praja Sahayaka Sewaya* (Community Assistance Service)', in *Environment and Urbanization*, Vol. 5, No. 2, October 1993.

Appendix 1

Sri Lanka: A situation analysis

1. General

'Sri Lanka is classified internationally as a "developing" country. My father read about this as a young man, now I read about it in my middle-age and my son reads about it in school', explains Nandasiri, a slum leader in Colombo. *'Yet, it is unclear to us what we, as Sri Lankans, want to achieve and how we want to define "development". Are the huge buildings and roads and the tourists on the seaside beaches indicators of "development"? Whose needs will be met by these?'*

Such questions illustrate the root of the growing Sri Lankan crisis. Yet, is it really a country in crisis? Sri Lanka has an impressive national record in social development which is often heralded as an example of development in the context of limited economic growth. Only 4 per cent of children die before their fifth birthday and infant mortality is on the decline, average life expectancy is 70 years and female literacy is said to be 85 per cent.

During the 1980s and early 1990s, despite its admirably educated workforce, opportunities in Sri Lanka have been limited and bouts of civil unrest have increased. Unemployment has exceeded 20 per cent of the labour force and there are sharp increases in the prices of food resulting from structural adjustments initiated by the IMF free market policies of the late 1970s. These have eroded the food security of the poor, and those who feel most alienated have resorted to violence and conflict as a means of settling grievances. The State has reacted by increasingly diverting resources into internal security.

It is a country now locked in a confusing array of extremes. It appears to the newly arrived visitor a tranquil setting, but its eruptions of violence defy this image. The opulence of 'Colombo 7' contrasts with the poverty of the majority who live in Colombo's slums and shanties. The ethos of the Buddhist majority obliged by faith to donate time and wealth to the poor is increasingly interpreted as an insult by many poor people who have been educated to view social welfare services as a legitimate right. Indeed, from 1935 until the 1980s Sri Lanka had strong Socialist and Trade Union movements.

2. The Socialist Movement: The politicization of the masses

Dr N.M. Perera (1934–79) was perhaps the most prominent political leader involved in the Socialist movement in Sri Lanka. Unlike most other intellectuals he was not content with merely analysing, interpreting and conceptualizing the reality of the world around him. He made a determined effort to transform the society in which he was born. It was N.M. Perera and other leftist leaders who led the national struggle for independence. Not content with mere constitutional reform with Britain, they demanded full national independence. Many were imprisoned but escaped to India where they joined the independence movement. They knew the Sri Lankan independence movement was greatly dependent on India's struggle.

The leftists also popularized politics, from an elitist activity to one involving the masses. They played an historic role in politically educating people from all social classes. One way in which this was done was by expressing modern political concepts in ways which could be understood by the people.

The Socialists' popularity with the masses made the government of the time wary. The government's strategic response was to use the provision of social welfare benefits as one means of diverting voters away from the Socialist left. Thus, during the 1960s and 1970s nearly 10 per cent of the annual Gross National Product went mainly on food subsidies, free education and health facilities. By any standards this is a sizeable level of welfare expenditure rarely seen in a country with the possible exceptions of some socialist countries.

The Socialists educated the masses to view welfare as their legitimate right and mobilized them to oppose any attempt to curtail services. In their political education, leftist politicians emphasized to the masses that the way to finance welfare measures is to transfer income from the rich to the poor by placing higher tax burdens on the rich, an approach which brought the notion of class struggle in an understandable way to the common man. Thus the Socialists functioned as a powerful pressure group in perpetuating resource commitments which led to Sri Lanka's high level of adult literacy and life expectancy. They also clearly played a vital role in developing the political consciousness of the increasingly educated poor majority.

3. The 1980s

The 1980s were a decade when Sri Lanka's progress in social development was significantly undermined. Prices began to increase in an unprecedented way: multiplying five-fold during the 13-year period from 1977–90. This has had devastating effects at the household level, especially for the poor who have few reserves and assets to fall back on.

During this same period social welfare expenditure by the government was drastically slashed. Per capita social expenditure dropped during the 1980s to pre-1960s levels. Concurrently, government expenditure on defence, public order and safety increased sharply from 1 per cent in 1982, to over 3.5 per cent by 1988.

The 1980s also saw the introduction of the government's new 'open door' policies. This created opportunities for contracts and commissions to be gained via large-scale development projects such as the Mahaweli. It also introduced tax concessions for established businesses, thus enhancing the wealth accumulation among the most prominent and powerful. The size, spread and magnitude of the black economy reached proportions previously unknown: estimated by the Minister of Finance in 1990 as equivalent to 20 per cent of the GNP (50 million Sri Lankan rupees).

4. Growing inequality

In Sri Lanka today there is a growing concentration of wealth in the hands of a few. This increasing inequality is all too evident to the poor who are politically astute and comparatively well educated. This is perhaps the greatest contributing factor to the current crisis in the country.

Sri Lanka now has one of the most unequal distributions of wealth in the world. Second only to Brazil (World Bank Report, 1990), 10 per cent of Sri Lanka's population enjoys 43 per cent of the country's income.

The progress of earlier years has faded. Sri Lanka today ranks among the poorest performers in the world when it comes to nutrition. There is no longer any significant difference in the nutritional status of children in Sri Lanka and children in the neighbouring countries of Bangladesh, India and Pakistan. Although the survival rate of Sri Lankan children is high, the quality of life of a substantial proportion of the surviving children is quite low.

5. Rural poverty

Sri Lankan rural communities are not homogeneous entities. The existence of

40

contradictions and conflicts, rather than harmonious interests, is a fundamental fact of life. In general, the basic village structure is characterized by the existence of dominant interests such as trader–moneylenders, landowners, rural elite and even rural bureaucrats. They benefit from the status quo. They also benefit from the poorer villagers who consist of the small and marginal farmers, landless workers, and rural artisans. In this context most rural institutions and so-called 'neutral' interventions in rural areas by government as well as NGOs become adjusted to the dynamic of these contradictions and end up benefiting the dominant interests and perpetuating the status quo.

While there is a conflict of interest and different classes and groups in rural areas, they are also mutually dependent on one another. These relationships take a dominant–dependent character or an unequal dependency relationship. The small commodity producer, whether a small farmer or rural artisan, for example, loses a considerable portion of his income to moneylenders, traders, land-owners, elite and bureaucrats through exorbitant interest rates and low terms of trade. Small farmers and artisans are often tied to the system in which they pay high prices for inputs and receive a low product price. This drain of the economic surplus through dependency linkages creates a process of impoverishment. It suppresses the poor and keeps the productivity of the rural economy at a low level.

These relationships also create dependency attitudes among the rural poor. Mental attitudes and value systems are created to legitimize the dependency relationships and perpetuate the social structure. Moreover, the poor themselves are not unified, being divided by the tradition of caste and recent systems of production. The poor often compete with each other out of necessity for the limited economic opportunities in the village. Dependency, attitudes and disunity inhibit many of the rural poor from taking initiatives. This in turn reinforces and stabilizes dependency relationships and the vicious circle of poverty it creates. This explains why it is difficult for self-reliant rural development processes to be spontaneously generated. A catalytic intervention is, more often than not, a necessary initial input for social mobilization; to support the poor to organize and take action to achieve self-reliant development.

6. Urban poverty

Dependency also characterizes the lives of the urban poor in Sri Lanka. Most urban low-income settlements (slums and shanties) initially developed around a small group of settlers, often a family or two of 'strong men'. They gained access to pieces of low quality government land, such as canal banks, road reserves and marshy areas. They began by putting up temporary houses. Other poor rural families hoping to find work in the urban areas then sought permission from the original families who asserted informal control over the area.

There are now 850 low-income settlements in the city of Colombo, with more than 350,000 residents. As these settlements have grown, new leaders have emerged, most often those with links outside the communities, to politicians and influential entrepreneurs. They often use their connections to protect the interest of the unauthorized settlements. Within any one settlement leaders may develop political ties to the ruling party as well as to the opposition parties. These are strengthened near election time and are used to ensure the settlement's chances of receiving government support. The residents may resent their leaders but support them nonetheless. There are often practical ties of dependency such as loans and marketing links. Dependent attitudes are also evident as leaders frequently build the hopes and expectations of residents for a better future.

In the late 1980s the government recognized the urgency of renovating the canal

41

system in Colombo. Without properly functioning drainage, the city would suffer increasingly from flooding by polluted waters. Hundreds of people who lived in canal bank settlements for decades were uprooted. This, and land shortage generally, is leading to poor people being resettled outside of central Colombo, often in marshy flood-prone marginal land far from markets and places of work. The already dire situation was made worse by the government's transport policy of 'people-ization'. This has been a privatization process of public transport which has led to a chaotic array of over-crowded mini-vans plying the streets during rush hour, and shortages of bus services during off-peak hours.

7. Women in poverty

The women's movement in Sri Lanka has had a limited effect on the rural and urban poor. It is of little consequence to these women that they have been allowed to vote since 1931 or that Sri Lanka produced the world's first female Prime Minister.

Poor women in Sri Lanka are co-earners in most families, primary earners in many families and sole earners in some households. The majority of these women are 'invisible' in that they are not part of the labour statistics. They are unprotected by labour legislation and trade unions. In contrast, the highly visible small number of professional women in Sri Lanka (11 per cent, 1981) has overshadowed the situation of the poor majority.

Although many poor Sri Lankan women, in both urban and rural areas, are main income earners it is seldom explicitly stated by her or her spouse. Most often such observations are expressed by neighbours. Authority, as an aspect of status, lies with the senior male adult. However, where the actions of behaviour of the male are perceived to fall short of the norm, women do take unilateral decisions, particularly with regard to taking up waged work if the husband, father or partner is not contributing significantly and regularly.

Regardless of how income is allocated within the household, it is the female spouse who bears the burden of housework and childcare. In situations where a woman perceives that her spouse is not fulfilling his ascribed role as a provider, and where women have access to their own income or support from kin, the most frequent method of bargaining is to refuse to cook food for him and to refuse to have sexual relations. Cooking and eating together in popular custom is the core of a *pavula* (union) particularly among Sinhalese. The refusal to cook for a husband is a veiled threat that he is no longer worthy of her total respect nor entitled to his rights as a husband.

Cultural norms dictate that women eat last and least. Their poor nutritional status has a direct effect on their children. Infant mortality rates of the urban poor range from 32–84 per 1000 live births, while the national average is 34 per 1000. In the rural areas, plantation workers' children suffer most with a crude death rate five times the national average. With the decreasing purchasing power of the rupee, the situation is only likely to worsen. Whereas food stamps in the 1950s were adequate for a month's supply of staple goods, food stamps by the end of the 1980s were only able to cover one-third of these costs. The scarcity and instability of income is forcing families to stop buying unperishable foodstuffs on a monthly basis, and is forcing them to purchase in small quantities, more frequently and at higher prices. The repercussions of this on the health of children is evident in Colombo where 25 per cent of children under six years of age exhibit signs of chronic malnutrition and 10 per cent of acute malnutrition.

For older children, birth order is significant in terms of responsibilities and contributions towards the functioning of the household. Older female children are expected to take more responsibility compared with older male children or younger siblings.

Appendix 2

The Women's Credit Union: Statistical overview, December 1994

Numbers of members in urban and rural locations

Urban areas

Location	Number of groups	Number of members
Colombo	91	745
Negombo	12	129
Dehiwala-Galkissa	9	74
Galle	14	133
Kotte	57	564
Kolonnawa	24	259
Peliyagoda	15	136
Moratuwa	4	28
Sub-total	226	2068

Rural areas

Location	Number of groups	Number of members
Maharagama	13	98
Kaduwela	6	58
Gampaha	37	335
Galle	23	191
Hanguranketha	25	195
Wariyapola	17	167
Dehiowita	4	40
Matale	5	56
Kekiriwa	5	50
Mahaweli	6	60
Boralesgamuwa	9	72
Kaluthara	25	238
Sub-total	175	1560
Total	401	3628

Appendix 3

The Women's Credit Union: Statistical overview of finance, December 1994

Savings and loans, Sri Lankan rupees (50 rupee = US$1)

Primary branch	Shares	Fixed term deposits	Compulsory savings	Children's savings	Loans issued	Loans collected
Bandaranayakapura	68950	1000	55930/43	7772/65	973932	935702
Bo Sevana/Gajabapura	119930	500	113571/57	31808/16	1028042	628869
13 & 15 Gardens	91060	3500	106855/00	20909/94	725005	352998
Bodhirajarama	33000		28071/59	5361/46	143605	64025
Seevalipura	33400		31542/19		348615	135547
Boralesgamuwa	12900		6565/00	150/00	136375	79375
Madiwela	12500		9919/00	8500/00	110725	55400
Kurunduwatta	57700	87500	51575/19	2802/14	336134	114876
U.E. Perera Mawatha	30000	5500	31226/52	9528/44	175688	62200
Bhathiya Mawatha	40050	1000	40685/59		348210	99549
Endera Mawatha	23640		8845/00	4330/00	82250	52660
Bollatha	41210		21500/00	685/00	347175	219650
Malwatta	30700	4000	24912/47	2375/00	280250	191560
Halmillewa	67100		55064/76	10188/60	629650	481496
Hanguranketha	16100		12901/50	955/00	209960	148550
Negombo	22200		7475/00		128625	92875
Velivitiya	5100		535/00	600/00	17000	13000
China Gardens	7600	500	1605/00		49875	27862
Total (rupees)	713740	103500	608780/81	105966/39	6071116	3756197
Total (dollars)	14,263	2070	12,176	2119	121,422	75,124

Appendix 4

The *Praja Sahayaka Sewaya* and the Million Houses Programme: Background information

Housing is at the heart of Sri Lankan politics, and indeed Sri Lankans generally perceive housing as one of their most fundamental rights. In April 1993, the Prime Minister announced the Million Houses Programme, a sequel to the Hundred Thousand Houses Programme (1978–83).

The objective of the new programme was to reach a larger number of households at a lower cost to the State but with a greater satisfaction to occupants. The major question was how to reach such a scale with limited finance and resources. After much consideration, the Government gave recognition to the fact that housing in Sri Lanka is an activity of the people and that the role of Government should not be to do what the people have been doing for centuries, i.e. building their own homes and settlements, but to strengthen this process by providing support where it is needed. The Million Houses Programme principles emphasized:

○ minimum intervention and maximum support by the State;
○ maximum involvement of the builder-family;
○ minimum assistance for many rather than ample assistance for few;
○ minimum standards for many rather than high standards for few;
○ decentralization of decision-making, planning and implementation to the local authorities, the communities and the householders.

The core of the programme was small housing loans to the rural and urban poor. Scale was essential in order to make a substantial and lasting impact on the housing situation, but scale could only be achieved through a devolved institutional structure. In the urban areas, the local authorities were expected to implement the programme through the municipal and urban councils, and through community development councils in the low-income areas.

Community Development Councils (CDCs) evolved through the practice of participatory delivery of urban basic services, with resource support from the United Nations Children's Fund (UNICEF). The aim was *'to wean the residents of urban low-income settlements away from a sense of over-dependency on external agencies and to develop confidence in their abilities to solve their own problems.'*[11] Although active during the Million Houses Programme, the CDCs' limitations became increasingly obvious. *'The structure did not encourage the community to become active in managing its affairs and maximizing its potential for self-development. The problems of working with the government bureaucracy were also apparent. Government staff have to work with administrative and financial rules and therefore were not able to respond to the pace of community activity.'*[12]

In 1986, the government's housing authority began utilizing community leaders to act as community assistants on the housing programme. These were individuals from low-income areas who had worked successfully within their own communities. The government asked them to carry out a programme to support small enterprises. Problems quickly developed between the needs and perspectives of the community assistants and those of the government staff. The community assistants began setting the seeds for forming their own autonomous organization, and in 1990 it was registered as the *Praja Sahayaka Sewaya*, a non-profit company.

45

Bibliography

ACHR/HIC, 1994, 'Finance and resource mobilization for low income housing and neighbourhood development: a workshop report', Pagtambayayong Foundation Inc., Philippines.

Anzorena, Jorge, 1994, 'Grameen Bank', *SELAVIP Newsletter*, October.

Anzorena, J., 1995, 'Catholic Social Services 1993–1994', *SELAVIP Newsletter*, April.

Cairncross, Sandy, Jorge E. Hardoy and David Satterthwaite, 1990, 'New Partnerships for healthy cities', in Sandy Cairncross, Jorge E. Hardoy and David Satterthwaite (Ed.), *The Poor Die Young: Housing and Health in Third World Cities*, Earthscan Publications, London, pp. 245–68.

Chambers, Robert, 1995, 'Poverty and livelihoods; whose reality counts?', *Environment and Urbanization*, Vol. 7, No. 1, April, pp. 173–204.

de Silva, G.V.S., et al., 1979, 'Bhoomi Sena: A Struggle for People's Power', in *Development Dialogue*, Vol. 2.

ESCAP, 1991, *Guidelines on Community Based Housing Finance and Innovative Credit Systems for Low-income Households*, United Nations, ST/ESCAP/1003.

Gamage, Nandasiri, 1993, '*Praja Sahayaka Sewaya* (Community Assistance Service)', *Environment and Urbanization*, Vol. 5, No. 2, October, pp. 166–72.

Hardoy, Jorge E. and David Satterthwaite, 1989, *Squatter Citizen: Life in the Urban Third World*, Earthscan Publications, London.

Hurley, Donnacadh, 1990, *Income Generation Schemes for the Urban Poor Development Guidelines* No. 4, Oxfam, Oxford.

Huysman, Marijk, 1994, 'Waste picking as a survival strategy for women in Indian cities', *Environment and Urbanization*, Vol. 6, No. 2, October, pp. 155–74.

Moser, Caroline O.N., 1987, 'Women, human settlements and housing: a conceptual framework for analysis and policy-making', in Caroline O.N. Moser and Linda Peake (Eds), *Women, Housing and Human Settlements*, Tavistock Publications, London and New York, pp. 12–32.

Moser, Caroline O.N., 1993, *Gender Planning and Development: Theory, Practice and Training*, Routledge, London and New York.

Patel, Sheela and Celine d'Cruz, 1993, 'The Mahila Milan crisis credit scheme; from a seed to a tree', *Environment and Urbanization*, Vol. 5, No. 1, pp. 9–17.

Pryer, Jane, 1993 'The impact of adult ill-health on household income and nutrition in Khulna, Bangladesh', *Environment and Urbanization*, Vol. 5, No. 2, October, pp. 35–49.

Sirivardana, Susil, 1994, 'Sri Lanka's experience with mobilization strategy with special reference to housing and poverty alleviation', Paper presented at the South Asian Regional Housing Conference, Colombo, June.

Tabatabai, Hamid with Manal Fouad, 1993, *The Incidence of Poverty in Developing Countries; an ILO Compendium of Data*, A World Employment Programme Study, International Labour Office, Geneva: Vol. 7, No. 2.

Tilakaratna, S., 1987, *The Animator in Participatory Rural Development*, World Employment Programme Technical Co-operation report, International Labour Office, Geneva.

UNCHS (Habitat), 1993, *The Urban Poor as Agents of Development: Community Action Planning in Sri Lanka*, Nairobi.

United Nations, 1995, *World Urbanization Prospects: the 1994 Revision*, Population Division, New York.

World Bank, World Development Report, 1990.

SMALL ENTERPRISE DEVELOPMENT
An International Journal

EDITOR-IN-CHIEF
Professor
Malcolm Harper

**CHIEF
CONSULTANT
EDITOR**
Jacob Levitsky,
formerly adviser on
small enterprise
development to the
World Bank.

Across the world there is a growing realization of the potential contribution of the small business sector to economic expansion and the achievement of improved living standards. *Small Enterprise Development* provides a forum for those involved in the design and administration of small enterprise development programmes in developing countries. It is genuinely international however, and news and views are welcomed from any source.

Small Enterprise Development contains:

- Detailed articles reporting original research, programme evaluations and significant new approaches.
- Case studies of small enterprise development projects implemented by donor agencies.
- Short practice notes from the various regions of the world describing programmes in operation and work of wider interest.
- Reviews of books, pamphlets and other material.
- News of projects and grants from the international and local agencies.

The journal tackles the major themes and pressing concerns of small enterprise development, such as technical assistance, finance for microenterprises, group co-operative enterprises, private sector involvement in enterprise development.

SUBSCRIPTION RATES 1997
Institutional rate £65 / US $110
Individual rate £38 / US $60

Small Enterprise Development is quarterly.

IT Publications Ltd

103-105 Southampton Row, London WC1B 4HH, UK.
Telephone: +44 (0)171-436 9761   Fax: +44 (0)171-436 2013
E-mail: itpubs@gn.apc.org
URL: http://www.oneworld.org/itdg/enterprise.html